Contents

Introduction

Aims of the guide

The purpose of this Student Text Guide to *Arcadia* is to enable you to organise your thoughts and responses to the play, to deepen your understanding of key features and aspects, and finally to help you to address the particular requirements of examination questions in order to obtain the best possible grade. It will prove useful to those writing a coursework piece on the play by providing a number of summaries, lists, analyses and references to help with the content and construction of the assignment.

It is assumed that you have read and studied the play already under the guidance of a teacher or lecturer. This is a revision guide, not an introduction, although some of its content serves the purpose of providing initial background. It can be read in its entirety in one sitting, or it can be dipped into and used as a reference guide to specific and separate aspects of the play.

The *Text Guidance* section examines key aspects of the play including contexts, interpretations and controversies. Emboldened terms within this section are glossed in *Literary terms and concepts* on pp. 104–10.

The final section, *Questions and Answers*, gives examples of essay questions of different types, and includes exemplar essay plans and samples of student work.

Page references in this guide refer to the 2000 Faber edition of the play.

Assessment Objectives

The Assessment Objectives for A-level English literature from 2008 are common to all boards:

AO1	articulate creative, informed and relevant responses to literary texts, using appropriate terminology and concepts, and coherent, accurate written expression
AO2	demonstrate detailed critical understanding in analysing the ways in which structure, form and language shape meanings in literary texts
AO3	explore connections and comparisons between different literary texts, informed by interpretations of other readers
AO4	demonstrate understanding of the significance and influence of the contexts in which literary texts are written and received

It is essential that you pay close attention to the Assessment Objectives, and their weighting, for the board for which you are entered. These are what the examiner will be looking for, and you must address them *directly* and *specifically*, in addition to proving general familiarity with and understanding of the text, and being able to present an argument clearly, relevantly and convincingly.

Remember that the examiners are seeking above all else evidence of an informed personal response to the text. A revision guide such as this can help you to understand the text and to form your own opinions, and can suggest areas to think about, but it cannot replace your own ideas and responses as an individual reader.

Text Guidance

Contexts

Life and works of Tom Stoppard

1937 — born in Czechoslovakia, second son of Martha and Eugene Straussler, doctor at Bata shoe factory

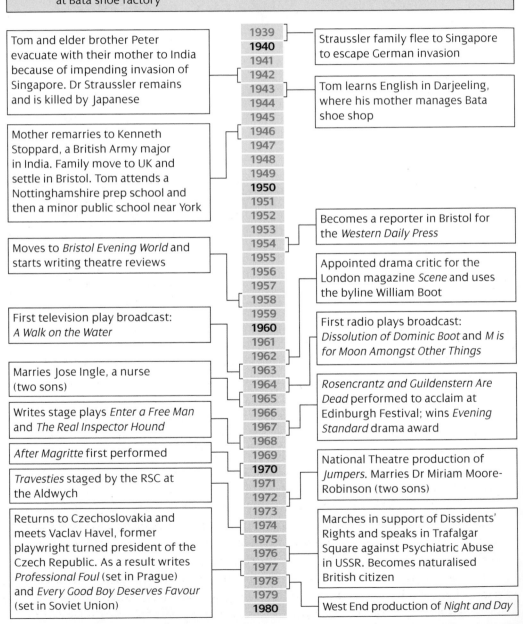

Tom and elder brother Peter evacuate with their mother to India because of impending invasion of Singapore. Dr Straussler remains and is killed by Japanese

1939
1940 Straussler family flee to Singapore to escape German invasion
1941

1942
1943 Tom learns English in Darjeeling, where his mother manages Bata shoe shop
1944
1945

Mother remarries to Kenneth Stoppard, a British Army major in India. Family move to UK and settle in Bristol. Tom attends a Nottinghamshire prep school and then a minor public school near York

1946
1947
1948
1949
1950
1951

1952
1953 Becomes a reporter in Bristol for the *Western Daily Press*
1954

Moves to *Bristol Evening World* and starts writing theatre reviews

1955
1956 Appointed drama critic for the London magazine *Scene* and uses the byline William Boot
1957
1958

First television play broadcast: *A Walk on the Water*

1959
1960 First radio plays broadcast: *Dissolution of Dominic Boot* and *M is for Moon Amongst Other Things*
1961
1962

Marries Jose Ingle, a nurse (two sons)

1963
1964 *Rosencrantz and Guildenstern Are Dead* performed to acclaim at Edinburgh Festival; wins *Evening Standard* drama award
1965

Writes stage plays *Enter a Free Man* and *The Real Inspector Hound*

1966
1967
1968

After Magritte first performed

1969
1970 National Theatre production of *Jumpers*. Marries Dr Miriam Moore-Robinson (two sons)

Travesties staged by the RSC at the Aldwych

1971
1972

Returns to Czechoslovakia and meets Vaclav Havel, former playwright turned president of the Czech Republic. As a result writes *Professional Foul* (set in Prague) and *Every Good Boy Deserves Favour* (set in Soviet Union)

1973
1974 Marches in support of Dissidents' Rights and speaks in Trafalgar Square against Psychiatric Abuse in USSR. Becomes naturalised British citizen
1975
1976
1977
1978
1979
1980 West End production of *Night and Day*

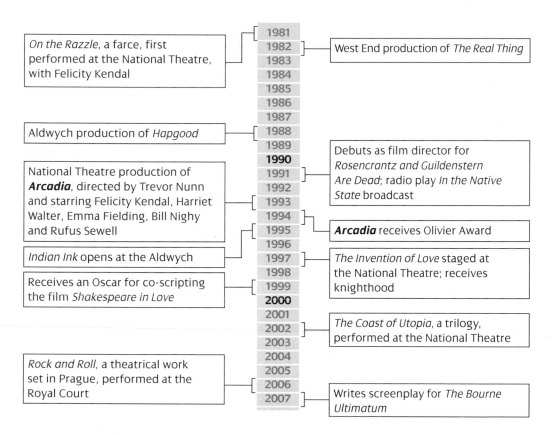

On the Razzle, a farce, first performed at the National Theatre, with Felicity Kendal	**1981** **1982** **1983** — West End production of *The Real Thing*
	1984 **1985** **1986** **1987**
Aldwych production of *Hapgood*	**1988**
	1989
National Theatre production of **Arcadia**, directed by Trevor Nunn and starring Felicity Kendal, Harriet Walter, Emma Fielding, Bill Nighy and Rufus Sewell	**1990** **1991** **1992** — Debuts as film director for *Rosencrantz and Guildenstern Are Dead*; radio play *In the Native State* broadcast
	1993 **1994**
	1995 — **Arcadia** receives Olivier Award
Indian Ink opens at the Aldwych	**1996** **1997** — *The Invention of Love* staged at the National Theatre; receives knighthood
Receives an Oscar for co-scripting the film *Shakespeare in Love*	**1998** **1999** **2000**
	2001 **2002** **2003** — *The Coast of Utopia*, a trilogy, performed at the National Theatre
	2004
Rock and Roll, a theatrical work set in Prague, performed at the Royal Court	**2005** **2006** **2007** — Writes screenplay for *The Bourne Ultimatum*

Sir Tom Stoppard as playwright

Stoppard is renowned for being an intellectual and wit who did not go to university but who is nonetheless a cerebral playwright whose erudition appeals to educated audiences. He has often been accused of caring more about ideas than about his characters. However, this claim is true of all **satirical comedy**, which by definition cannot allow the audience to feel sympathy for victims of fate and error, only scorn for the institutions and **stereotypes** they represent. There is, in fact, a **pathos** and poignancy about some of the younger Stoppardian characters and their situations, which contrasts with the savage ridicule of their elders, supposed betters, and employers. Stoppard has also often been criticised for gender bias, though given the topics and settings of his plays — which have tended to focus on all-male or male-dominated institutions — it is unsurprising that he has included relatively few significant female characters, and this is in any case not true of *Arcadia*.

Stoppard always researches the background theories for his plays extensively (something that he claims he owes to his training as a journalist) and has sometimes been inspired with an idea for a play by his reading matter. He often rewrote or adapted his works for a different genre: for example, *Indian Ink* (1995) was an adaptation of his radio play *In the Native State* (1991), and his television play *A Walk on the Water* (1963) became the stage play *Enter a Free Man* (1968). He wrote the screenplay as well as the original theatre script for *Rosencrantz and Guildenstern Are Dead*, and throughout his career has moved with ease between the media of radio, television, stage and film.

Though Stoppard claims to be politically non-aligned, his sympathies in his work and life have always been directed towards talented individuals and against systems and regimes. He is on record as saying he found public school life a negative influence, and other repressive institutions that have been the butts of his satire are the House of Commons, Oxford University, British Intelligence services and the police force, as well as colonialism (India), totalitarianism (Czechoslovakia/USSR) and the Denmark of *Hamlet*'s Claudius. He viewed Vaclav Havel, another Czech playwright born one year earlier than himself, as his mirror image, the one who failed to get away and achieve political and artistic freedom.

Felicity Kendal

Stoppard lived with the actress Felicity Kendal for eight years from November 1990 after their respective divorces. They met on the set of *On the Razzle* in 1981, when she was a 'pert actress with an alluringly husky voice'. It is unclear whether they ever married before they split up in 1999. Since he wrote several of his middle-period works, starting with *The Real Thing* (1982), with her in mind as the lead female character, her influence on his work is significant, especially since he had been previously accused of not writing strong enough parts for women. Kendal was previously a comic television actress best known for her leading role in *The Good Life* (1975–78). The wholesome decency, idealistic passion and ironic perceptiveness of that role are clearly recognisable in the character of Hannah Jarvis.

Influences

The influence of minimalist Samuel Beckett (1906–89) and the Theatre of the Absurd is noticeable throughout Stoppard's work, but particularly in the early plays. *Rosencrantz and Guildenstern Are Dead* (1967) has many echoes of Beckett's *Waiting for Godot* (1952) (e.g. the pair of bewildered main characters, the **stichomythic dialogue** and the metaphysical speculations). Stoppard was also attracted to **surrealism**, and in fact one of his early stage plays was called *After Magritte* (1970), in which the curtain opens on a ludicrous tableau of a man dressed in what appears to be a ballet tutu standing on an ironing board with his hand in the air, watched by a suspicious policeman through the window. (The character is in fact changing a light bulb, while preparing for a ballroom dancing party, and there is a perfectly rational explanation for all the apparent absurdities.)

Jumpers (1972) contains a team of acrobats in yellow suits, a hare shot by an arrow and a squashed tortoise, but generally the elements of surrealism and **farce** in Stoppard's later works are inherent in the more subtle linguistic rather than the visual medium. There is nothing bizarre about the appearance of characters or props in *Arcadia* (other than, perhaps, the pet tortoise-cum-paperweight) but many of the exchanges of dialogue are comically surreal.

As a postmodernist writer, Stoppard has written plays that predictably defy categorisation as either comedy or tragedy, since they are a mixture of moods and **genres**, contain fiction and non-fiction, self-referential and **intertextual allusions**, shifts of time and viewpoint, and emphasise structures and parallels. Unpredictability is the unsettling undercurrent in all his plays, highlighting the limitations of science and knowledge and therefore of our ability to control our public and private lives. However, irreverent humour alleviates the seriousness of these weighty concerns.

Arcadia

James Gleick's *Chaos: Making a New Science* (1987) and the discovery of Chaos Theory (as expressed in the statement 'A butterfly stirring the air today in Beijing can transform the storm systems next month in New York') gave Stoppard the idea for the story of *Arcadia*. It is likely that he also read Mandelbrot's essay of 1992 on 'Fractals: a geometry of nature'. He found that the fascinating subject of fractal mathematics provided a powerful **metaphor** for human behaviour.

Stoppard believes *Arcadia* to be one of his best plays, as 'things intersect properly'. The play originally ran for three hours and ten minutes and had to be cut, which Stoppard found very difficult: 'You try to write it in a way that makes it impossible to leave anything out, or you haven't written it properly. Then you find you have to leave something out.'

The satirical novels of Thomas Love Peacock, who is referred to and quoted from in the play, and particularly *Headlong Hall*, appear to have influenced the setting, content and **characterisation** of *Arcadia*. In Peacock's novel a collection of guests at a country house includes a vitriolic reviewer, a best-selling novelist, a poet and a landscape architect. *Arcadia* also shares remarkable similarities with *Possession* (1990), the novel by A. S. Byatt, which oscillates between the present day and the Victorian era and concerns two literary sleuths trying to establish that there was a secret relationship between two poets.

A debt to Oscar Wilde is apparent in this play in that not only is much of the dialogue **epigrammatic** and interrogatory but Lady Croom bears a close resemblance to Lady Bracknell, the amusing, opinionated, fearsome dame of *The Importance of Being Earnest* who has an ineffectual and absent husband. Wilde's play is quintessentially about grand families, country houses, social mores and sexual propriety, making it a direct descendant of Shakespeare's comedies, a forerunner of twentieth-century sit-coms and a model for *Arcadia*.

Regency England

George III, the third of the Hanoverian (German) kings of Great Britain, ascended the throne in 1760. Although he lived until 1820, he suffered from intermittent mental illness, and on several occasions Parliament transferred the monarch's powers to his son, the future George IV, to act as Prince Regent. From 1810 onwards, this arrangement became permanent, and this period, which came to be known as the Regency, coincided with a major upsurge in cultural life. The word 'Regency' came to be synonymous with elegance, refinement, style and taste.

Although there are no directly political references in *Arcadia*, Stoppard has chosen to place the play in this period because of its cultural and artistic milieu, which acts as the background to the action. It marks the cusp between Classicism and **Romanticism**, as well as the turning point between two widely different views of the role and nature of gardens (see *Gardens and landscapes* on p. 20). The period is also marked by a number of prominent sexual scandals, several of them relating to Lord Byron.

England and France

England and France were seriously at war throughout the period covered by the earlier plot-line (April 1809 to June 1812), and the discussion of French and English algebra needs to be seen against this background. The Napoleonic War was the largest-scale war on the European continent undertaken by England since the fifteenth century, and there was a clear political dimension: monarchical England was fighting against a revolutionary France that had executed its king, Louis XVI, in 1793 and replaced him with a revolutionary government led by Napoleon. There was widespread fear among the British upper classes of a popular uprising in Britain in sympathy with the 'fashion for godless republicanism' (p. 54). Lady Croom describes Europe as being in 'a Napoleonic fit' and points out the dangers of travelling to France at this time.

Literary magazines

Regency England saw the heyday of literary magazines, published in either London or Edinburgh, the earliest of which dated from the mid-eighteenth century. They typically included anonymous reviews, often highly venomous. A critical industry has grown up in recent years, which attempts to identify from internal evidence some of these contributors, who undoubtedly included most of the leading literary figures of the time. Some of the most famous of such magazines were the *London Magazine* and the *Edinburgh Review*, which was founded in 1802 by Francis Jeffrey. The *Piccadilly Recreation* is a fictional name; Byron's actual review of Wordsworth appeared in the July 1807 issue of *Monthly Literary Recreations*.

Duelling

Duelling (in theory to the death) was a long-established activity between nobles, and increasingly gentlemen, as a way of resolving a quarrel, often over a woman, or dealing with an insult. The practice harked back to medieval jousting. Although not declared illegal until 1819, it was frowned upon at the time of the play, and the police would bring a prosecution for murder in cases of the death of a participant. To ensure secrecy, duels took place at dawn in remote places, and if one of the parties was killed, the survivor would flee the country to avoid punishment. Seconds were the men who controlled the timing and distance and arranged the choice of weapons, originally swords and later pistols. There are documented examples of duels occasioned by rivalries that arose from the publication of opposing views in literary magazines. The example cited by Bernard in Act 2 scene 5, where the poet Tom Moore challenged the critic and editor Francis Jeffrey in 1806, was in fact interrupted by the police before any violence could be done, and it turned out that at least one of the pistols was empty (see p. 70). A duel was allegedly fought by two novelists defending respectively the **classical** and Romantic literary approaches. By the time of the play it was an archaic practice; this explains the ridicule with which Septimus greets Chater's demand for 'satisfaction'.

The suggestion that the historical Byron might have been prepared to participate in a duel is not far-fetched: his great-uncle killed his cousin, Mr Chaworth, in a duel over a dispute at cards, and Byron himself is said to have come close to participating in one with a captain in Malta in September 1809 — although there is no evidence that he actually did so.

Expeditions of scientific discovery

The expedition to Martinique, the island in the West Indies on which Ezra Chater receives a monkey bite and conveniently dies (p. 119), is but one of many that were being mounted in the early part of the nineteenth century for the purpose of discovering and naming new species of plant and animal. A full-blown national passion for botany developed, which culminated in Charles Darwin's celebrated voyage on the *Beagle* to the Galapagos islands, providing him with the evidence for his theory of evolution and transforming the intellectual world of the Victorians. Dahlias originated in Mexico and had first been brought to Europe at the end of the eighteenth century — the fruit of another voyage of scientific exploration — but the dwarf dahlias sent by Captain Brice would have been the first of their kind in Europe, hence Lady Croom's delight in being the first to show one.

Country houses and architecture

In the Middle Ages, the lord of the manor of each English village lived in a fortified manor house. As time passed, the fortifications gave way to increasingly imposing houses, which reinforced the local status of their owner. It was not until the eighteenth century, though, that it became fashionable to employ architects to design what came to be known as 'country houses', many of which were built onto or around an earlier building. As part of the classical movement of the eighteenth century, houses in the 'Palladian' style, which reflected the serene classical perfection of the Italian architect Andrea Palladio (1508–80), were very much in vogue. They were characterised by a classical facade displaying symmetry, harmony and balance, with Ionian porticoes and pediments. These houses were also typically surrounded by carefully landscaped gardens, formal and symmetrical, which were based on those of the sixteenth-century French palaces, such as Versailles, which were in turn based on Roman models, or the more natural mid-century designs of 'Capability' Brown and his followers (see *Gardens and landscapes* on p. 20).

Country life

Travel was by coach or on horseback, and slow. It would have taken several days, for instance, for Lady Croom to go to London. This was partly the reason why house guests stayed for a long time compared to the modern practice of a visit to friends or relatives; several weeks or even months was not uncommon. Being cut off from neighbours and towns, and with few diversions, country-house owners encouraged guests, especially those with an amusing talent, those who were famous or fashionable, or those who would make up a shooting party or ride to hounds. Piano playing was regarded as a useful accomplishment for entertainment purposes. Without electricity and dependent on candles (which were expensive), even the wealthiest inhabitants of country houses rose early and retired early to bed, fitting their activities into the hours of daylight.

The lady of the house, not having even sport as a hobby and confined to the house, passed her time in music, dancing and other social and artistic pursuits. She would expect to spend the social season in Bath or London, where she would attend plays and art exhibitions, the main aim being to be seen in public doing the latest things wearing the latest fashion, rather than to improve her education. Unlike the sons, who were sent away to public schools at the age of seven, the daughters would be tutored at home, usually by a governess, and were not expected to become proficient at anything more than the usual domestic accomplishments of sewing, drawing, singing, their designated future role being to catch a husband and look after his house and entertain his guests. It was considered dangerous to over-educate a female child, as this would render her unmarriageable, and advantageous marriages for daughters were the basis of the continuation of the aristocratic system.

The age of 'coming out' (i.e. of making a debut at a ball to announce her availability for suitors to make an offer to her father for her hand in marriage) was 16, hence Lady Croom's concern with Thomasina's age. By the age of 20 a woman was considered to be a spinster and likely to become an old maid. Needless to say, a young female was chaperoned on the rare occasions she was allowed out in public, as her reputation (a **euphemism** for virtue or chastity) was her chief asset — along with her dowry. This puts in context Thomasina's shockingly forward behaviour with Septimus and raises the question of why she has a male tutor in the first place, since this was extremely rare. One can only guess that he was really hired for her mother's benefit, as it was a **cliché** that affairs occurred between mistresses and male employees as well as between masters and maids. (Branwell Brontë was a tutor who got himself into such a situation with a Mrs Robinson of Thorp Green.)

Eldest sons (younger ones had to go into the church and navy respectively) automatically inherited their father's estates (and usually his full name as well) and were expected to involve themselves in politics as a way of ensuring the continuation of the family's privileges and interests. The lords of the manor, apart from engaging in hunting, shooting and fishing, did very little, as they had stewards to see to the running of the estate, grooms to look after the horses and stables, and gamekeepers, stewards and servants galore to do all the work required for the upkeep of the house, garden and estate. When fashions in architecture or landscape demanded it, an expert would be brought in to redesign the house or garden, to add a wing or to cut down an avenue of trees.

Queen Victoria and the Victorian age

The accession to the throne of Queen Victoria in 1837 marked a turning point in the fortunes of the British monarchy. Ruling for 64 years (she just survived into the twentieth century), she gave stability following the failings of her predecessor. Her long reign gave its name to a distinctive period in English history during which the foundations of the modern world were laid. Science and technology transformed everyday life, but they also transformed intellectual life, finally eclipsing religion as the leading influence when the fruits of Charles Darwin's voyages of discovery were published in his masterwork *The Origin of Species* (1853) and a fatal wedge was driven between science and Christianity. It was a period marked by grief as well as doubt, as the queen's beloved husband Albert died when she was only 42; the nation was plunged into mourning and the queen wore black for the remainder of her reign.

The Victorian age was also known as the Age of Progress. Almost free of war for the British, exceptional economic growth was matched with extension of parliamentary democracy, significant improvements in living conditions, and legislation to protect the rights of the less fortunate members of society. A new style of architecture emerged — Victorian Gothic — and in literature there were great novelists (the Brontës, George Eliot, Dickens and many others) and poets (Tennyson especially, the poet laureate who followed Wordsworth and was a favourite of the queen). It was also the period when the British Empire reached its greatest extent and power, and Queen Victoria became Empress of India.

The Victorian period had a strong influence on many aspects of British life. Although *Arcadia* is set both before and long after the Victorian era, some of the characters from the early period lived on into Victoria's reign. The hermit did not die until three years before Victoria's accession, and the articles discussed by Bernard and Hannah in *The Cornhill Magazine* date from the high Victorian period; the magazine was not founded until 1860, with William Thackeray as the first editor, and continued to be published until 1975. In some ways Thomasina can be seen as an echo of Alice, the precocious young girl immortalised by the Oxford mathematician C. L. Dodgson in *Alice's Adventures in Wonderland*. The play introduces and prefigures many of the social and intellectual debates that would continue to rage throughout the century.

Classicism versus Romanticism

By setting the play in 1809, Stoppard can chart the changing climate of ideas at the turn of the nineteenth century, when there was, according to Hannah, a 'decline from thinking to feeling' (p. 37). The two systems of thought of Classicism and Romanticism can be said to have used the western artistic canon as their battleground ever since. They are fundamental oppositions in literature, and a way of distinguishing and discriminating between people, actions, attitudes and settings.

In *Arcadia* these antagonistic stances of style, taste and temperament are reflected in the characters, in their studies and pursuits, and in the changes to the garden. **Romanticism** is a layer imposed on top of Classicism, like the before and after versions of the landscape, so that the two movements can be viewed and compared. Typically, reason was attributed to the male of the species, and emotion to the female, which makes it amusingly anti-stereotypical that Hannah is the rationalist and Bernard the Romantic. Septimus and Thomasina rise above both modern-day characters by being able to cross the divide and comprehend and apprehend both ways of viewing the universe.

The Enlightenment

Also known as the Age of Reason, the Enlightenment refers to the period from the early eighteenth century to the French and American revolutions in the 1770s and 1780s, a period that embraced the **classical** influence of rational order and natural law. It was also called the Augustan period because key authors were explicitly trying to imitate the eminent writers, such as Horace and Virgil, who flourished during the reign of the Roman emperor Augustus. The term 'classical' embraces nostalgia for and emulation of the literary practices and social values of Greek and Roman antiquity. These include the belief that only the intellect can raise us above an existence otherwise indistinguishable from that of animals, who live by their instincts and appetites. The crucial tenet of neoclassicism was the understanding of the universe through the application of reason, free from superstition and scepticism, with a strong emphasis on knowledge; the goal was freedom and happiness, but within the social contract between the individual and the state. Elegance of expression and control of form were highly regarded as civilised virtues, and universal concerns were considered more enduring and important than those pertaining to the individual. As Dr Johnson said: 'the business of a poet […] is to examine not the individual but the species […] he does not number the streaks of the tulip.'

The aim of classical writing is usually didactic rather than affective, hence the tendency towards the well-tried formulae of satirical polemical essay, ode and (mock) epic, which favour balance, conventional imagery and abstract nouns. It is also associated with comedy, in which restraint, balance and harmony are paramount considerations. Unlike Romantic ones, classical texts do not normally include references to animals, women, children or peasants, as for them the proper study of man was man as a political being, and his role in the community and public life. Their contexts, therefore, are usually urban and contain dialogue, debate and rhetoric as dominant devices. Many late seventeenth- and eighteenth-century works are in classical mode, such as those of Milton, Swift, Pope and Jane Austen.

The Romantic movement

Variously defined as the period from 1790 to 1820, or the 50 years from 1775 to 1825 (or even as late as 1837, the year of the accession of Victoria to the British throne), Romanticism was a revolt against the rationalism of the **Enlightenment**, rejecting precepts of order, harmony and restraint and instead embracing the individual and the imaginative, the spontaneous and the visionary, the original and the mystical, the non-conformist and the rebellious. Excess replaced balance, the organic replaced the mechanical, as neoclassical values were rejected as insincere, impersonal and artificial in all aspects of culture. The emotions and senses were considered superior to the intellect, and applied particularly to the beauties and changeable moods of nature. Rapture, melancholy, sentimentality, nostalgia and horror were the extreme feelings to be cultivated. Romantics believe that not everything can or should be explained by logic or science, and that some mystery should be left in the world because the imagination needs to feed on magic and fantasy to be able to create. Childhood was revered as a time when susceptibility to emotion and wonder are at their strongest. Feelings, because intuitive, were to be trusted rather than thoughts, which can be regulated, and impulses followed were considered safer than rules obeyed. Bernard is a Romantic in his belief in his gut instincts and disregard for evidence.

Genius loci and hermits

The concept of the *genius loci* (Latin for 'spirit of the place') has a long ancestry, going back to the **nymphs** and **satyrs** of classical mythology and the belief that the god Pan inhabited the landscape and caused the noon-day panics to which he gave his name. This **pantheism** links Ancient Greece with the Romantic era and the Romantic era with the contemporary academic research into the history of the garden, layering the three historical eras, many centuries apart, that are represented in the play.

Poets had sublime status in the early nineteenth century, after Shelley and Coleridge had conferred upon them quasi-divine powers of perception and creation; they revived a **Gothic** and supernatural worldview and were fascinated by death and violence; they preferred to be outdoors and wrote about scenery and ruins, the grandeur of lakes and mountains and forests, and the spirits that haunted them and provided inspiration to humans; they revered Nature as a divine force and believed that those who cut themselves off from man's roots in the countryside would perish spiritually. For them a hermit was a man in the ideal state of natural innocence, essential wildness at one with untamed wilderness. Hermits and anchorites have bibilical **connotations** (see Thomasina p. 19 on John the Baptist) as well as Romantic literary ones; Heathcliff in *Wuthering Heights* is an eremitic type, and there is a sage hermit in Coleridge's *The Ancient Mariner*. Such figures were generally associated with insanity, as well as intuitive wisdom, as solitary existence tends to produce that effect or it is given as an explanation for seeking such a way of life.

Because everything is in a state of flux, and therefore happiness, youth, beauty, innocence and emotions are ephemeral, it is necessary to *carpe diem* and snatch fleeting pleasure from the jaws of time. Because of the inevitability of loss, pain, physical decay and old age — unless pre-empted by an early death — the Romantic mode is a tragic one. Thomasina and Septimus both have Romantic ends, early death in the flush of youth and decline into isolation, grief and madness being typical fates for those — and not only in literature — who dare to pursue forbidden knowledge or to experience the full taste of life.

Byron and the Romantic poets

Byron was the most flamboyant and notorious of the second generation of Romantic poets born at the end of the eighteenth century. Born in 1788, the son of an impoverished Scottish heiress, Catherine Gordon, and a fortune-hunting widower, John 'Mad Jack' Byron, George Gordon became sixth Lord Byron of Rochdale and heir to Newstead Abbey in Nottinghamshire in 1789. At Cambridge he enjoyed sport, theatre, gambling and dissipation, and suggested by his numerous and various affairs that he was bi-sexual. Having been born with a club foot made him sensitive to criticism and determined to compensate in the fields of love and literature. He was vain and had a horror of getting fat, which made him often starve himself, which in turn made him bad-tempered. He took offence easily and was involved in a street brawl with a dragoon in Pisa in May 1822.

Mysterious disappearance

In March 1809 he published anonymously *English Bards and Scottish Reviewers*, a **satire** of contemporary poets and playwrights. In April there are a few days unaccounted for in his biography. In July he set sail from Falmouth to Lisbon and travelled in Southern Europe: Portugal, Spain, Greece, Albania, Turkey, Malta and Gibraltar. Though going on the **Grand Tour** was common enough among young gentlemen at the time, he was not able to go to the usual countries because of revolutionary fervour in Northern Europe, and posterity has been unable to uncover his reasons for leaving the country so suddenly and spending two years abroad when he had just turned 21 and therefore had the right to take up his seat in the House of Lords. However, the crumbling ancestral pile of Newstead Abbey and his profligate lifestyle were plunging him into debt, and his first book of poems, *Hours of Idleness*, had been sneeringly received, hence the satirical response of *English Bards and Scottish Reviewers*.

1809 had certainly not been a good year for Byron: two of his friends had met with fatal accidents; a servant he had seduced had become pregnant; his beloved dog Boatswain had died and he had written an extended and moving epitaph for him. He turned a human skull into a drinking vessel and announced in a letter to his solicitor John Hanson on 16 April that there were 'circumstances which render it absolutely indispensable, and quit the country I must immediately'. 'I will never live in England if I can avoid it' he wrote from Albania. 'Why, must remain a secret.' He was avoiding his creditors, fleeing from depression and indulging his travel lust, but some critics feel there must be more of an explanation. One has offered Byron's fear of being given the death penalty for sodomy and his need to exchange furtive homosexual affairs in England for the more erotically tolerant climate of Greece. Whatever the reason — and duels were often the cause of hasty departures from English shores — he was back in the country and womanising by 1811.

Fellow poets

Most of his fellow poets did not think particularly highly of Byron, nor he of them. He openly mocked Southey, poet laureate from 1813–43, whom he detested for his extreme Tory politics and his limited literary talent; in his long ironic dedication to Southey in **Don Juan** (1819), he called him 'insolent, narrow and shabby'. His comments on Keats were personal and deeply offensive: 'There is no bearing the drivelling idiotism of the Mankin' and 'Such writing is a sort of mental masturbation — he is always frigging his Imagination'. Byron also insulted Wordsworth in *English Bards and Scottish Reviewers* (1809, but subsequently withdrawn by him), referring to his 'prose insane', and his scathing review of Wordsworth appeared in the July 1807 edition of *Monthly Literary Recreations*. Byron was friendly with the Shelleys, however, and it was while they were staying with him and his lover, Mary's half-sister Claire (Jane) Clairmont, in the Villa Diodoti on Lake Geneva in the summer of 1816, that Mary Shelley wrote *Frankenstein* as her contribution to the ghost-story competition set up by Byron. After Shelley's death, Byron wrote to his publisher John Murray: 'You were all mistaken about Shelley, who was without exception, the best and least selfish man I ever knew.' Shelley had always been generous with his praise for Byron's work, especially *Don Juan*.

Lady Caroline Lamb

Byron's poetic work of 1812, *Childe Harold's Pilgrimage*, was the story of his two-year sojourn abroad. It was a runaway success and created the new **stereotype** of the Byronic hero, which was attractive to women. Later that year he had a scandalous affair lasting four months with Lady Caroline Lamb, whom he then rejected after having almost eloped with her. She spent the next four years pursuing him shame-lessly: she stalked him, she dressed as a page, was put in a straitjacket, starved herself and attempted suicide. Married in 1805 to the Whig prime minister Viscount Melbourne, 'Caro' was a high-profile figure in London society, having been born into the aristocracy in 1785. She included a description of her relationship with Byron in her **Gothic** romance *Glenarvon* of 1816, and thereafter published a further two novels and two narrative poems, mostly anonymously. She is popularly believed to have died of a broken heart in 1828 after a breakdown precipitated by seeing Byron's funeral cortège in London in 1824. She it was who famously described Byron as 'mad, bad and dangerous to know'.

Ada Lovelace

In 1813 Byron had an affair with his married half-sister, Augusta Leigh, which resulted in a daughter. Two years later he married 'Annabella' Milbanke (1792–1851) and they had one child, Augusta Ada Byron (1815–52), who became Countess of Lovelace on her marriage and was Byron's only legitimate child. Thomasina is modelled on the historical figure of Ada Lovelace, who was a math-ematical prodigy and who worked under the inventor of the idea of a programmable computer, Charles Babbage (1791–1871). Byron dubbed her mother Annabella, also mathematically gifted, his 'Princess of Parallelograms'.

Untimely death

Byron's marriage to Annabella was a disaster and a year later, in 1816, Byron abandoned his family, went to Europe and never returned. In 1822 he received the heavy blow of the news of the death of his natural daughter by Claire Clairmont, Allegra, at the age of five. Three months later he learned of the tragic drowning of Shelley in the Gulf of Spezia in Italy; he attended his funeral pyre on the shore near Livorno (then known as Leghorn).

For the next two years Byron travelled around, writing poetry and falling in love, until he became involved in supporting Greece in its War of Independence against the Turks. Though he suffered from various ailments, including rheumatism, biliousness and epilepsy, and had at one stage travelled with a personal physician (John Polidori), his death at the age of 36 was not caused by any of them. He died in April 1824 at Missalonghi, an unhealthy swampy region of Northern Greece, as a result of excessive blood-letting by leeches as treatment for a fever, probably malaria. This medical malpractice was exactly the same as that which later killed his daughter Ada, and at the same age. Like Ezra Chater's cause of death, Byron's was not Romantic — and could even be described as **bathetic** — except in being premature, in an exotic location and while acting as a revolutionary. His body was returned to Nottinghamshire and put in the family vault in July 1824, after burial was refused at Westminster Abbey.

The Byron legacy

Byron's life and death collected myths, so much so that his friends campaigned to sanitise his reputation *post mortem*. His executors burned the manuscript of Byron's memoirs, according to his will instructions. Thomas Moore wrote an official **biography**, published in 1830–31, that was very tactful. In addition to his **poetry, he** is remembered by the worldwide Byron Society, to which Bernard and Hannah refer, for his dietary fads, his bathing habits, his musical box and his limp. He represents for a wider audience a contradiction of two frames of reference, having been adopted by both **classical** and Romantic sympathisers. His preference for eighteenth-century satirists and his personal poetic style, with its robustness and regularity of rhyme and metre, ally him to the former, and his *Don Juan* of 1818–19 is a mock-epic that ridicules **Romanticism**. Bernard claims him as a rationalist and admires him accordingly, though ironically he is not one himself. Byron had nothing but contempt for aesthetes and self-indulgent sensual verse, but on the other hand he is the epitome of Romanticism — hence the coining of the term Byronic — with his trauma, his dark looks, his rebellious-ness, and his pursuit of physical danger and gratification, like the questing heroes and lovers of his poems. So much has he always been seen as the 'bad boy' of English literature that he was not granted a funeral plaque in Westminster Abbey until 1969.

The *Arcadia* Byron

In *Arcadia* Byron's presence, defined by his absence, in 1809 is in the role of a would-be wit and would-be seducer, but at this stage he has not written his defining works, and Stoppard seems to be ironically subverting his later stereotypical image and reputation as a womaniser and author by making him weak and unsuccessful in every way: he does not succeed in bedding more than the easy-virtued Mrs Chater; he is a poor shot and unsafe with firearms; he is criticised by Septimus for his poor ability in Latin; he is derogatorily called 'facetious' by Augustus

(p. 106) and considered not a gentleman for claiming the latter's hare, and he manages to offend his hostess to the point of getting himself ignominiously thrown out of Sidley Park.

With the exception of Bernard, it is only women in the play who are impressed by him; by 1812 Thomasina is saying (p. 105):

> He is the author of *Childe Harold's Pigrimage*, the most poetical and pathetic and bravest hero of any book I ever read before, and the most modern and the handsomest, for Harold is Lord Byron himself to those who know him, like myself and Septimus.

Her enthusiasm may be saying more about her fantasies than about Byron, however, and she may be deliberately trying to annoy her mother and to make Septimus jealous.

Lord Byron and his mystery cause the revelation of the great divide in temperament and approach to scholarship between Bernard and Hannah, as well as being the missing link to all the other characters in the play. His work is quoted twice, once in scene 5 by Bernard to show how beautifully he wrote:

> She walks in beauty, like the night
> Of cloudless climes and starry skies,
> And all that's best of dark and bright
> Meet in her aspect and her eyes

and once by Hannah in scene 7 to reveal an uncannily relevant description of the heat going out of the world:

> I had a dream which was not all a dream.
> The bright sun was extinguished, and the stars
> Did wander darkling in the eternal space,
> Rayless, and pathless, and the icy earth
> Swung blind and blackening in the moonless air

Byron therefore lends himself to both the art and the science of the play.

Gardens and landscapes

Country houses in England are a consequence of the feudal system, which was the economic model that operated throughout the Middle Ages and later. Nobles held large areas of land, given to them by the king, in return for supplying soldiers for the royal army as needed. They in turn gave parcels of their land to lesser nobles and knights, who gave their personal military service as payment. In this way, every village had a 'lord of the manor' (often a knight, who was not technically a lord) who lived in a manor house. The relatively humble, and often fortified, dwellings of the Middle Ages were rebuilt as country houses from the Tudor period (fifteenth century) onwards. Significant areas of land were attached to each of these houses, much of which was (after the Middle Ages) leased to tenant farmers, but a part of which remained under the direct control of the owner.

By the early nineteenth century, the time in which *Arcadia* is principally set, the vast majority of agricultural land in England was still owned by great and middling landowners. When the vogue for professionally designed gardens came to Britain in the eighteenth century, part of the owner's estate was taken out of cultivation and converted into a garden for pleasure and leisure, and simply to be seen and admired. The importance of the garden and landscape in *Arcadia* is entirely typical of the way that country-house owners felt at the time. The changes were more than changes of fashion; they represented social, political and cultural upheaval and the dominant thought of the day, Augustan and then Romantic.

The first wave of garden design, in the seventeenth century, had been inspired by the formal gardens created in the sixteenth and seventeenth centuries in France, most famously at Versailles. These in turn drew heavily on Roman formal gardens and were inspired by themes from classical antiquity. This style showed respect for the monarchy, history and ancient institutions of England. Highly regular, they celebrated man's dominance over nature; beauty lay in the geometry of circles (pools) and lines (paths), and in the symmetry of flower beds and the intersections of hedges (artificially shaped by topiary), alleys and terraces. Fountains and statues were considered *de rigueur* as a homage to classical figures and designs. All of these features were later rejected as Frenchified and constraining.

The three phases

In the early eighteenth century, the previous artificiality was superseded by landscape designs drawing heavily on the classical landscapes painted by the two great French landscapists of the seventeenth century, Nicolas Poussin (1594–1665) and Claude Lorrain (1600–82). Gardens of this period are characterised by the careful placing of statues and classical temples in the landscape, but formal symmetry was banished. William Kent (1685–1748) was the leading English designer, and his gardens at Stowe are perhaps his most celebrated. At Rousham House in Oxfordshire he created a sequence of Arcadian set-pieces punctuated with temples, cascades and Palladian bridges.

By the middle of the eighteenth century, there was a reaction against the formality and artificiality of even these designs, led by the most famous of English garden designers, Lancelot 'Capability' Brown (1716–83) (so nicknamed because he flattered landowners by stressing the 'capability' of their estates to be improved). Brown's landscapes offered harmony and expansiveness; his gardens were more 'natural', with asymmetric designs incorporating lawns, clumps of trees and lakes, the latter being typically irregular in shape (usually serpentine) and with islands. Brown often undertook substantial earthworks in order to create the 'natural' effect he was seeking. Humphry Repton (1752–1818), who continued this approach after Brown's death, was celebrated for his use of 'Red Books', which showed 'before and after' views of a garden by the use of overlays. A feature of gardens of this period, and viewed by Brown as essential, was the 'ha-ha', a sunken ditch that acted as a physical boundary between the garden and the countryside beyond, but which, being invisible, allowed the vista to stretch uninterrupted into the distance. This idea is based on Rousseau's championship of the superiority of the natural over the man-made in a complete change of attitude to Nature; now the goal was that gardens should imitate untamed countryside, devoid of walls, fences, hedges and other artificial barriers to open prospects.

By the end of the century there was a further reaction and another phase to landscaping. As Romantic ideas developed, the belief arose that gardens should be 'wild', 'picturesque' and 'romantic', which involved destroying Brown's carefully planned gentle undulations and harmonious views and replacing them with something closer to chaos. The picturesque style combined ancient with modern, had roughness and irregularity, and turned neglect into an art form. The paintings of the Italian Salvator Rosa (1615–73) provided examples of wilderness upon which some designers explicitly based their gardens. Unlike the formal and the natural gardens, both waiting to be contextualised and populated by human figures on public view, the picturesque garden was secretive and anti-aristocratic, pandered to a vogue for melancholy, mystery and reverie, and acknowledged the value of privacy and solitude, the interior rather than the public life; it was the final shift from reason to imagination.

Sidley Park

Sidley Park and its 500 acres have undergone all the transformations to which fashionable estates were subject during the eighteenth and early nineteenth centuries and constitutes a palimpsest of the main styles of garden design, the evolving landscape architecture reflecting the social changes. 'The house had a formal Italian garden until about 1740', as Hannah tells us (p. 31). Then, under the influence of 'Capability' Brown and others, including Humphry Repton, an asymmetrical natural look of sinuous curves and informal clumps of trees was introduced: 'the whole sublime geometry was ploughed under by Capability Brown' (p. 36). As *Arcadia* opens, this is about to give way to Mr Noakes — the 'Emperor of Irregularity' — and his picturesque style of wilderness and broken lines and jagged shapes ('and then Richard Noakes came in to bring God up to date', p. 37).

He is still there, and the project far from finished, in 1812. Lady Croom appears to be mocking him and his style when she asks him to provide a hermit, but in fact owners of grounds in the new picturesque style often did install hired recluses in their grottoes, with stipulations concerning their clothing, the length of their hair and the observation of silence. (Many of them found the imposed solitude and uncomfortable cave conditions unattractive, and one was caught at the end of three weeks going to the pub.) By now Noakes has, much to Lady Croom's annoyance, acquired a steam pump. Thomas Newcomen (1663–1729) invented the first atmospheric steam engine in 1712. The invention marked an important early stage in the development of the Industrial Revolution, because it meant that power could be made available anywhere (previously it had been dependent on harnessing running water, which severely restricted the location of factories). Noakes's pump is used to drain the lakes at Sidley Park, but its intrusive noise is symbolic of the brutal intervention of human science to destroy 'nature as God intended', as Lady Croom puts it (p. 16).

Arcadia

'**Arcadia**' is a curious and complex concept. It appears to refer to an actual place in Ancient Greece, but in reality it is a place of the mind, a romantic invention that never existed in the real world and arguably never could have done. It recalls that earliest of imaginary pastoral paradises, the Garden of Eden. The history of the Arcadia fiction could serve as a paradigm for the development of the European intellectual tradition, of which it forms an important part in that it brings together the **classical** and Christian traditions and fuses both their images of utopia: it imports the serpent into the garden.

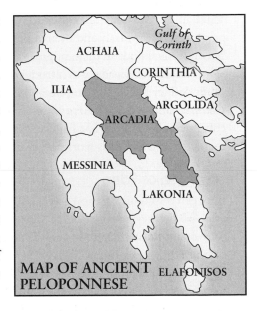

MAP OF ANCIENT PELOPONNESE

Classical Arcadia

Arcadia was originally simply the name of a region of the Peloponnese in southern Greece. A long way from the culture of the Athens of Pericles, it was largely composed of barren mountains and was home to a few shepherds in classical times. Its principal claim to fame was as the birthplace of the god Pan, the god of nature. Pan was a creature of **paradox**: his upper half was human and cultured, and he famously played the pan pipes, while his lower half was that of a goat, the animal famed in myth for uncontrollable lust, and his pipes were principally used to attract **nymphs**, whom he then seduced. Also named after him is the idea of 'panic' — an irrational fear that originally overtook victims caught outside in the middle of the day, in rural and secluded places in Greece or what is now Italy (see E. M. Forster's short story *The Story of a Panic*). With the later identification of Arcadia with Eden (see p. 24), Pan became the classical equivalent of the serpent in the garden, representing lust and sin in paradise.

Virgil's Arcadia and the Renaissance

The great Roman poet Virgil is responsible for our modern conception of Arcadia. When he wanted a setting for his **pastoral** poems about happy shepherds, gods and nymphs, *The Eclogues*, he chose to place them in 'Arcadia', an area of Greece which he had certainly never visited but which, because of its remoteness, no one could say was not as Virgil described it.

In common with much else from Greek and Roman antiquity, Virgil's Arcadia was rediscovered during the Italian Renaissance and came to be a dominant theme in much sixteenth- and seventeenth-century painting. The Neapolitan Jacopo Sannazzaro (1458–1530) wrote an influential book entitled *Arcadia*, published in 1504 in Venice, and thereafter **idylls** with shepherds and nymphs were widely employed, first in Italy and then in France, where the works of Claude Lorrain and Nicolas Poussin made them popular and familiar.

The idea of Arcadia was introduced to English literature in the 1580s when Sir Philip Sidney began work on his ambitious prose idyll *Arcadia* (later known as *The Countess of Pembroke's Arcadia* after its dedicatee), which concerns a romantic chivalric quest as an escape from and contrast to the debased life at court, a popular theme in Shakespeare's work and that of his contemporaries.

The Garden of Eden

Between the classical period and the Renaissance, European culture was profoundly affected by the introduction of Christianity, which rapidly became the dominant religion on the continent and constituted the subject matter of most of the painting during the Middle Ages.

The Christian equivalent of Arcadia was the Garden of Eden — a pastoral paradise, but one quite different from Virgil's: there were no shepherds or nymphs, no music and no sporting gods or goddesses, just one very stern one. The prototype humans, Adam and Eve, were introduced into this paradise, along with a serpent (Satan in disguise) who succeeded in turning the humans from their intended (by God) path, as a result of which they were expelled from the Garden, forfeited their immortality, and they and their descendants were sentenced to a life of toil.

This archetypal story of **the Fall** led to a set of iconographical and literary images and **themes** that have permeated European literature: the apple, the serpent, the tree, the temptation, the judgement, the expulsion. As shown by Milton in *Paradise Lost*, the precise crime of Eve, under Satan's baleful influence, was to eat the fruit of the Tree of Knowledge, i.e. to seek to know more than had been decreed. There are inherent paradoxes involved in the Fall, however, including the issue of how Eve, created as an afterthought and with an inferior intellect to her pre-existing male mate, could have been expected, in her state of unsuspecting innocence, to recognise and defeat the wily power of Satan, leader of the rebel angels and king of Hell, especially when he was disguised as a snake. The fact, or fiction, remains that the final fruit of Eve's disobedience was to bring death into the world, and it is with seduction and death that apples, and women, have since been associated.

'Et in Arcadia ego'

Although this Latin phrase seems to be redolent of classical antiquity, it is actually unrecorded prior to the sixteenth century. It is first found not in a literary text but in a celebrated painting by Guercino, in which a pair of Arcadian shepherds find a skull (a **memento mori**) resting on a wall with the inscription '*Et in Arcadia ego*' carved into the stone. This initial **juxtaposition** of the words with death makes their original meaning clear and renders much of the subsequent debate about meaning otiose, although it is nevertheless instructive to trace its development.

Although Latin is now rarely taught, for nearly 2,000 years it was the common language of European scholarship, and all educated people could be expected to be familiar with it. This phrase, however, is grammatically slightly tricky because it contains no verb and appears to literally mean 'And in Arcadia I'. More accurately, however, 'et' should be translated 'even', so the original meaning is: 'Even in Arcadia, I am to be found'. The 'I' clearly refers to death, and the sentiment is the simple one that, even in Paradise, death is the fate that awaits all of us (and is clearly the meaning of Joshua Reynolds's little-known etching on this subject).

Guercino's painting was a commission by Giulio Rospigliosi, the future Pope Clement IX, a well-known humanist and Latin scholar, and it has been suggested that it was the latter who actually coined the phrase. The painting has always been in Rome (in the Galleria Corsini) and clearly provided the inspiration for Poussin's first attempt at the theme. Painted in about 1630, it shows four shepherds finding a tomb in Arcadia, on the top of which a skull (reminiscent of Guercino) is clearly visible. But it was Poussin's second, mature working of this theme (*The Arcadian Shepherds*, 1637–39) that was to propel it to the forefront of artistic and literary consciousness — and at the same time to muddy the meaning of the words and their connection to the original idea. For although a tomb is being examined in *The Arcadian Shepherds* there is no skull, no obvious melancholy, no suggestion of the presence of death — indeed, the presence of the young nymph might suggest quite the opposite. It is surely this highly popular painting that appeared to legitimise the alternative but inaccurate translations of the phrase, which rely upon a grammatical inversion. To read it as 'I, too, am in Arcadia' (whether the speaker is the dead person in the tomb, an observing shepherd, the painter, or even, as Lady Croom suggests (p. 16), a viewer of the painting) is simply wrong, thus serving as an example in the play of false belief.

It is perhaps worth mentioning what is almost certainly an intellectual 'hare', probably started by Dan Brown, the author of the multimillion-selling novel

The Da Vinci Code. In it he suggests that '*Et in Arcadia ego*' is actually an anagram for '*I! Tego arcana Dei*', meaning 'Depart! I conceal the hidden things of God'.

Stoppard's '*Et in Arcadia*'

So why is Stoppard's play about literary detective work across the centuries, or about fractal mathematics and thermodynamics, or about sex and literature, called *Arcadia*? Partly it is to draw attention to the role played by the Sidley Park garden, never seen but a permanent presence just offstage. It sets the scene, provides the setting for much of the action and is a symbolic representation of many things. Stoppard's Arcadia fuses the two related concepts of pastoral paradise: classical by name but Christian by adoption. The Arcadia of the title is both a literal garden (subject to considerable and controversial meddling as various fashions compete for its soul) and a metaphorical Eden from which various characters find themselves expelled and where the pursuit of the fruit of the Tree of Knowledge leads to death.

On one level, the park represents the battle between classical and Romantic notions of whether humans should control and manipulate landscape and the countryside, but it also represents the flawed nature of Paradise: Satan and sin are also in the garden. When Lady Croom says 'Here I am in Arcadia, Thomasina', she is drawing attention to the idyllic role that an English country-house garden was supposed to play, and at the same time ironically reminding us how far this garden falls short of Paradise.

Coming of age in the garden

The relation between country-house gardens and coming of age through sexual awakening, and hence the loss of innocence of childhood, has been a popular literary theme for nearly two centuries. In medieval literature a similar symbolism was attributed to the walled garden as female sexuality, owned by her husband, with the locked gate representing chastity, and the presence of an interloper an attack on her virtue. This usage of the garden setting can be found in Chaucer, Spenser and Shakespeare. In Victorian literature, such as *Alice's Adventures*, the summer garden is suggestive of illegitimacy, secrecy, fecundity, alternative reality, and all that is outside the controlled boundaries of regular and acceptable social conduct. Among many more recent examples, L. P. Hartley's *The Go-Between* (1953) chronicles the coming of age of a young boy through his involvement in the illicit love affair between a tenant farmer and the daughter of the country house on whose estate the boy spends the overheated July days leading up to his thirteenth birthday. Similarly, in Ian McEwan's novel *Atonement* (2001), the peace of a languid June day in the classical gardens of the Tallis house is shattered by a young girl's disastrous interference in the affair between her sister, the elder daughter of the house, and the son of a former servant. In these literary examples the garden represents a non-innocent nature that actively encourages sexual congress across the class divide, deceiving and damaging the immature onlookers and leaving them disturbed, guilty and loveless for life. It cannot be coincidental that it is the adolescent Thomasina who asks the naive question that reverberates through Sidley Park and down the ages.

Science, art and nature

The central matrix of *Arcadia* concerns the complex pattern of relationships between maths, science, logic, philosophy, creativity, the Creation, music, literature and art. Stoppard sees culture as a seamless web embracing all knowledge and he is interested in the ways in which the strands of the sciences and the arts intertwine. In the great 'Two Cultures' contest, Science and Art stand in opposing corners of the boxing ring, as Bernard reminds us. But as many have pointed out, and as Stoppard is doing in *Arcadia*, it is not as simple as that, and the dividing line is sometimes hard to draw. Is a piano less of a machine or a tool than a steam engine? Does one have greater value to society than the other? Is Septimus the **classical** language scholar and literary reviewer less admirable than Septimus the mathematician, and is Thomasina the sketcher of hermits and tortoises less interesting than Thomasina the student of iterative functions? Not only can these judgements not be absolute, but they beg the question of whether scientific and artistic talents are in fact so distinct. Music is famously both an application of mathematical principles as well as a product of inspiration and imagination, and mathematicians have always claimed that solutions have harmony and beauty. In the medieval period, music was thought to represent the sound of the heavenly spheres in movement, i.e. to be a divine and natural rather than a man-made phenomenon. In the play, 'spotting the tune' and 'noise' are analogies made between music and the interpretation of mathematical data.

Natural phenomena

Where nature fits into the scheme of things is a fundamental question being asked by this play (as indeed it is in Shakespeare's). Perhaps the opposition is not between Science and Art at all, since both can be described as artificial and abstract in relation to the living original, but between Science and Nature. In *Arcadia*, however, Thomasina and Valentine use algorithms to attempt to establish mathematical equations for natural phenomena, such as leaves and grouse populations, i.e. they are using statistics to understand nature, thereby proving the numerical basis of creation. The borders between science and nature and art are shown to be permeable ones, as when Valentine chides Hannah (p. 62) that the leaf she is holding would become 'a mathematical object' if subjected to iterated algorithms, and when Thomasina and Augustus are given a still-life drawing task in scene 7 that consists of 'geometrical solids', a pyramid and a cone, juxtaposed with a pot of dwarf dahlias.

Earlier (p. 59) Valentine says that maths and nature have developed unpredictably and in an interrelated way:

> …it had been the same maths for a couple of thousand years. Classical.
> …Nature was classical, maths was suddenly Picassos. But now nature is having the last laugh. The freaky stuff is turning out to be the mathematics of the natural world.

Studying animal population data through a computer is like putting 'nature in a box'. Thomasina, inspired by an apple leaf, understands that 'forms of nature must give up their numerical secrets and draw themselves through number alone' (p. 56) and that the same laws apply to both bells and bluebells.

Mixed minds

Through the play's **characterisation**, Stoppard suggests that while one aspect of skill and knowledge may be dominant, it is human nature to show leanings in both directions, to reconcile the apparent dichotomy between science and art, sense and sensibility. Even Chater manages to be both a poet and a botanist, occupations normally considered mutually exclusive. The only character determined not to show any interest in or sympathy for science is Bernard, and this is presented as arrogance and a character weakness for which he is punished. The play itself refuses to accept that there is a boundary between art and science, or even between **Romanticism** and Classicism. When he tells Hannah that she is not enough of a Romantic to make a heroine out of Caroline Lamb and should study Byron instead, Bernard is actually revealing the limitations of his own mind. Genius transcends the limitations of subject specialism and compartmentalisation, and the greatest thinkers of classical times and the Renaissance — Leonardo da Vinci, Aristotle, Chaucer — dabbled in areas of knowledge far removed from their ultimate claim to fame.

Lost and regained

Where disciplines might arguably differ is in the ease or possibility with which lost knowledge can be found again. Septimus tries to persuade Thomasina that all the knowledge in the book treasures burned in the great library of Alexandria will resurface one day; the corkscrew could have been reinvented and, as the play shows, fractals and iterative functions and Fermat's theorems and any number of mathematical and scientific breakthroughs could and would be rediscovered.

This is, however true of scientific ideas, not convincing as an argument when applied to the arts and unique creations of an individual imagination: 'the missing plays of Sophocles' (p. 50) will proabably not turn up, and if they are 'written again in another language' (p. 51), they will be different plays. This is one of the fundamental differences between science and art, fact and fiction, and either Septimus wants to believe, like Valentine, that personalities do not matter, or he wants to console Thomasina.

Fermat, Newton and Mandelbrot

Pierre de Fermat

Pierre de Fermat (1601–65) was a French mathematician with a particular gift for developing new theorems. He was principally responsible for the development of modern Number Theory and of calculus. Frustratingly, he rarely provided proofs of his theorems, although all of them have subsequently been proved to be true. Some scholars suspect that he was deeply intuitive and had not actually proved them at all; this is most likely the case for the celebrated 'Last Theorem'. In 1637 he scribbled a note in the margin of his copy of the *Arithmetica* of Diophantus:

> I have a truly marvellous proof of this proposition which this margin is too narrow to contain. (Original Latin: 'Cuius rei demonstrationem mirabilem sane detexi. Hanc marginis exiguitas non caperet.')

The theorem may be stated in a number of forms, but the most succinct is:

> If an integer n is greater than 2, then the equation $a^n + b^n = c^n$ has no solutions in non-zero integers a, b and c.

It was to be 357 years before Fermat's Last Theorem was proved, and the complexity of the eventual proof, employing whole categories of mathematical reasoning developed only in the twentieth century, suggests that Fermat was not telling the whole truth. (As the proof runs to dozens of pages, it would have to be an exceptional margin to hold it!)

Andrew Wiles

Andrew Wiles was born 1953 in Cambridge, educated at Oxford and Cambridge Universities, and was appointed professor at Princeton University in the USA in 1982, aged only 29. He made the solution of Fermat's Last Theorem his life's work, and it took him 25 years to achieve it. For seven of those years he lived as a virtual hermit in order to concentrate on the task. He used the Taniyama–Shimura Conjecture as the basis of his approach, but developed it in new directions.

He finally announced his solution in a series of lectures in June 1993, but it turned out that there was a flaw in the proof that he had not noticed, and finally it was not until September 1994, and after help from a co-worker, that he had a moment of inspiration, which enabled him to complete the solution.

Simon Singh wrote a best-selling book about Wiles and his solution entitled *Fermat's Last Theorem* (1997) (*Fermat's Enigma* in the US edition), based upon a documentary film of the same name made by him in 1996.

Fermat and *Arcadia*

The proving of Fermat's Last Theorem, ironically the year after *Arcadia* was first performed, aptly illustrates Stoppard's point in the play that as time moves on lost knowledge is rediscovered, as new genius — and technology — replaces the old and adds another layer to human endeavour, experience and achievement.

Fermat is introduced as early as page 4 of the play, but only as a rather desperate attempt by Septimus to divert Thomasina's attention from the more interesting issue of 'carnal embrace'. Although Thomasina is a brilliant mathematician, there is no suggestion that she actually gives any attention to the problem; she dismisses Fermat's marginal claim thus: 'The thing that is perfectly obvious is that the note in the margin was a joke to make you all mad' (p. 8). However, the story clearly appealed to her, because we learn at the beginning of scene 4 that she rather facetiously prefaces her *New Geometry of Irregular Forms* with the words 'This margin being too mean for my purpose, the reader must look elsewhere' (p. 56).

Newton's Laws of Motion

Isaac Newton (1642–1727) was one of the greatest scientific minds of the seventeenth and eighteenth centuries. He is best known for developing the Universal Theory of Gravitation, but he also stated that three fixed mechanical laws could account for all the movement in the universe. He believed the physical laws of the universe were orderly, predictable and best expressed in mathematical form. One consequence of these mechanistic laws was that, in principle, all future events could be predicted if one had sufficiently complete knowledge at any one point in time. These laws were the basis of the 'Newtonian' view of the universe that held universal sway until Einstein's Theory of Relativity displaced it in the early twentieth century.

The view that all events can be predicted according to physical laws is known as '**determinism**' and conflicts directly with the Christian view that humans have **free will**. If they do, then their actions cannot be mechanistically predicted; if they do not, then the entire religious edifice of holding people morally responsible for their actions must fall. This conflict between free will and determinism has occupied many of the finest philosophers throughout history.

It is introduced into the play in scene 1, when Septimus summarises Thomasina's question thus: 'If everything from the furthest planet to the smallest atom of our brain acts according to Newton's law of motion, what becomes of free will?' (p. 7). Thomasina prefers to express it: 'If you could stop every atom in its position and direction, and if your mind could comprehend all the actions thus suspended, then if you were really, *really* good at algebra you could write the formula for all the future' (ibid.) This perception, which Septimus states to be a new insight of Thomasina's, remained valid until the early twentieth century when Werner Heisenberg, in his celebrated Uncertainty Principle, stated that it was impossible fully to measure the characteristics of sub-atomic particles, and therefore that the kind of complete description of all the particles in the universe suggested by Thomasina is impossible, and not merely in practice but in principle.

Second Law of Thermodynamics

Thermodynamics is the study of heat and temperature in relation to the mechanical power produced. Heat is a form of energy and temperature is a measure of hotness. The first law states that interaction between two bodies creates a heat in exact proportion to the work done to create it, thereby maintaining an equilibrium.

The Second Law postulates that the process cannot be reversed, i.e. that heat cannot be turned back into work and that energy cannot be transferred from a cooler body to a warmer one. An important implication of the Second Law, which was not immediately apparent, is that loss and decay are universal trends in nature, and that there is a one-directional passing of time. This is the idea, which came to be known as 'entropy', that everything in the universe is moving towards a less ordered state. It therefore follows that the universe will grow old and die, exemplified by the way in which a star eventually loses its heat and light and is extinguished.

A string of European physicists and mathematicians were involved in the exploration of thermodynamics during the nineteenth century. Baron Jean-Joseph Fourier (1768–1830) derived a 'Heat Equation' from Newton's law of cooling, which was an early step in the development of the second law. When Septimus mentions the 'prize essay of the Scientific Academy in Paris' (p. 108), he is referring to Fourier's Heat Equation. The French scholar Nicolas Sadi Carnot (1796–1832) first enunciated the Second Law, and it was developed by the Germans Hermann von Helmholtz (1821–94) and Rudolf Clausius (1822–88). The latter actually introduced the idea of 'entropy' in 1865 to summarise the irreversible nature of heat flow, introducing the idea that the entire universe is inevitably tending towards extinction. Another way of describing this idea is the 'Arrow of Time', i.e. that time can only move in one direction and that actions cannot be reversed, a term coined by the British astronomer Arthur Eddington (1882–1944) in 1927.

The emergence of Chaos Theory

Mathematics has developed significantly with the introduction of non-linear applied mathematics. Whereas hitherto it was supposed that linear equations sufficed, and that two and two made four, we now realise that extraordinarily complex behaviour can be generated by the simplest of rules, deriving not from complex causes but from a simple algorithm working chaotically. Early 1970s' studies of fluctuations in animal populations were the launch for 'chaos mathematics'. In Newton's system, time was not active and equations worked just as well in reverse. The science of heat and energy, the thermodynamic approach, however, gave time a direction, and thereby an ending. Newtonian physics provided an ordered and deterministic view of the world, but it could not explain the randomness and unpredictability of some phenomena. It became clear that complex patterns, such as the weather, could not be described by simple equations; even relativity and quantum theory can only explain the very big or the very small, and this leaves out most things.

During the 1970s 'Chaos Theory' was developed by mathematicians in an attempt to model hitherto unpredictable phenomena, using non-linear equations; clouds, snowflakes and thunderstorms all seemed to follow Nature's laws rather than Newton's. Chaos theorists postulated that in many systems a small change in the original conditions could create vast changes in the whole system; an example frequently given of this idea was that a butterfly fluttering its wings in Brazil could cause a hurricane in Texas. Other systems particularly affected by Chaos Theory are the economy and evolution. The first and most influential book to bring these ideas to the attention of the general public was *Chaos: Making a New Science* by James Gleick, published in 1987.

Mandelbrot sets

The Polish-French mathematician Benoît Mandelbrot (born 1924) was almost single-handedly responsible for popularising 'fractals'. These are actually iterative mathematical functions, but when plotted as a graph, and with colour employed to highlight the detailed working of the function, they created a new art form. The nature of an iterative function is that any point can be chosen and fed back into the equation, creating a new image, a process that can continue infinitely. Apart from their inherent beauty as forms, the most interesting feature of fractal images is how remarkably some of them approximate to complex shapes in nature, such as the patterns of leaves. The group of images derived from Mandelbrot's functions are known as 'the Mandelbrot set'. When, therefore, Thomasina says 'I will plot this leaf and deduce its equation' (p. 49), she is being presented as a mathematical pioneer of fractal images. When, in scene 7, Valentine shows Hannah 'the Coverly set', it is in direct homage to Mandelbrot, and the process he describes on p. 101 ('Each picture is a detail of the previous one') is replicating Mandelbrot's process. This is, of course, a fiction: there is no evidence that anyone understood the potential of recursive and iterative functions in the nineteenth century.

Mandelbrot summarised the relationship between mathematics and nature, in his introduction to *The Fractal Geometry of Nature*, thus: 'Clouds are not spheres, mountains are not cones, coastlines are not circles, and bark is not smooth, nor does lightning travel in a straight line.' So, when Thomasina says 'Mountains are not pyramids and trees are not cones' (p. 112), this is a cheeky intertextual and anachronistic pre-echo of Mandelbrot by Stoppard.

Population biology and the science of complexity

This is the study of the structure and behaviour of biological communities as ecosystems. In particular, it attempts to monitor, and mathematically model, the rise and fall of animal populations in relation to food supplies, mating and predation. A number of complex variables are at work, including species interaction and the environment. It was scientists working in this field who were among the first to see that Newton's laws did not apply here. However, the mathematics of chaos and iterative functions turn out accurately to model natural phenomena of this kind. In the play, Valentine is using data on the population of grouse on the estate over nearly 200 years to illustrate his theories of population biology. This is one of a number of new sciences that have resulted from the development of Chaos Theory. The use of complex computer modelling, relying on new programming algorithms and huge increases in computing power, allow vast quantities of data to be processed, and a new understanding has emerged of phenomena such as the behaviour of birds in flight and global climate patterns.

Arcadia and science and mathematics

An important **theme** of *Arcadia* is the unexpected interrelatedness of science, theoretical mathematics and nature. The Second Law of Thermodynamics, describing the fundamental nature of the universe, was developed by mathematicians, Chaos Theory being really a mathematical model. Mandelbrot's fractals prove Thomasina's conjecture that all natural phenomena, however complex, have a mathematical equation that describes them; and then those same iterative functions prove to accurately model (and therefore predict) extremely complex phenomena in the natural world, as Valentine demonstrates.

Mathematics plays a key and central role in the play, which has two mathematicians (one a 13-year-old prodigy) as central characters. Leaves, grouse and clouds are all imbued with the grandeur and magic of maths in the play. Septimus sets Thomasina to solve Fermat's riddle as a way of keeping her quiet, but later her investigation into the Second Law of Thermodynamics, and into the relationship between geometry and nature, lead her into important theoretical areas. After her early and tragic death, Septimus dedicates the remainder of his life — having retreated to Noakes's hermitage and become 'the hermit of Sidley Park' — to attempting to complete Thomasina's proof. The implication of the Second Law of Thermodynamics that disorder will increase until all energy is dissipated and all life extinguished is a bleak prognosis. It hangs heavily over the play in both the 1809 and the 1812 scenes (and is reflected even in a poem of Byron's), but is redeemed by the parallels and similarities with the present age, which suggest that all is not lost, and that the energy and the enthusiasm of the young will eternally rejuvenate the world. It is a fascinating fact that although the historical Byron had no interest in such matters, his only legitimate child, Ada Lovelace, was a remarkable mathematical prodigy, and it seems likely that Stoppard based Thomasina at least in part on her.

The debate between free will and determinism remains as lively today as it was in the nineteenth century, and an interesting new dimension to our notions of causation was introduced with the development of Chaos Theory in the 1980s. We now tend to believe that a situation can be both determined and unpredictable (a conclusion arrived at earlier in the century by Heisenberg), though not random, hence the paradox of 'deterministic chaos'.

Scientific ideas never stand still, and in the 1960s James Lovelock introduced what he called the 'Gaia Theory', arguing that in some respects the planet can be seen as a self-regulating mechanism that has self-organising recuperative properties. This has been adopted by some observers as a counter-argument to entropy, as it suggests that time's arrow can be swung to point in the direction of continuing creation.

Scene summaries and notes

The schoolroom setting and props are the same throughout. The final scene has the modern characters dressed up in the period costume of the Regency characters, thus conflating the two time periods in the same place and in the same month of June.

Act I scene 1

10 April 1809

Thomasina and Septimus are in the schoolroom discussing 'carnal embrace' and it emerges that Septimus has been caught in the gazebo by Noakes, indulging in this activity with Mrs Chater at her request. Thomasina's interest is diverted to solving Fermat's Last Theorem as a maths exercise, while Septimus hopes to be left in peace to read Chater's *The Couch of Eros*, which he has been commissioned to review (Septimus's review of *The Couch of Eros* will be published on 30 April 1809). Jellaby comes with a letter challenging Septimus to a duel from Chater, who then arrives in person. The letter is put into *The Couch of Eros*. Septimus distracts him from his ire about his wife with disingenuous flattery of his poetry, as an ironic result of which Chater inscribes Septimus's copy of *The Couch of Eros*, in the hope that he will review it kindly, not knowing that Septimus has previously condemned his earlier work, *The Maid of Turkey*, in his brother's publication, *The Piccadilly Recreation*. Lady Croom enters with Brice and Noakes in tow. The latter produces his sketch book, which includes a design for a hermitage. There follows a discussion of the garden and fears that it will be destroyed by Noakes and his new ideas. Brice sees Augustus shoot a pigeon, though Lady Croom attributes the shot to Byron. When her mother and her 'troops' have left, Thomasina draws a hermit on the sketch. She then gives Septimus a note from Mrs Chater, which begs him to deny everything, and this is also put into *The Couch of Eros*.

This scene introduces language and concepts that will recur, in particular the link between making love and making discoveries, both of which can come about by accident or mistake. Carnal embrace is important to the play as a whole because it is a reference to the Fall of man and to Thomasina's move from innocence to experience, as is reinforced by mention of '**free will**', 'God's will' and 'Sin' on p. 7; her increasing knowledge of science and maths is paralleled by her increasing knowledge of sexuality, as revealed by her reference to seed and **Onan**. 'Knowing' in the Bible is a **euphemism** for sexual intercourse. The dissemination of knowledge has thus started at the very beginning of the play, and as Thomasina points out, it is Septimus's job as her tutor to 'teach [her] the true meaning of things' (though ironically the roles are actually reversed, and already Septimus is being startled and led by Thomasina's thinking, as shown by his pause on p. 7). She is equally interested in what is for dinner and is childishly ('goody') pleased to discover that it is rice pudding. That she addresses her tutor by his first name is very unusual for the period, and suggests her precociousness as well as his unconventionality. Science and art are introduced and intertwined in this first scene, the links being landscaping and the studies of Thomasina.

Noakes's sketch book is described in the stage direction as imposing 'after' over 'before' views of the landscape, with the comment that '*Repton did it the other way round*'. Since the audience know neither that Noakes is '*an admirer of Humphry Repton's "Red Books"*' nor that he reversed the normal pattern, an **allusion** and thematic point available only to the reader is lost to the audience, as so often in the play. Thomasina's proleptic creation of a hermit of Sidley Park (inspired by the many picturesque paintings of John the Baptist in the wilderness that existed at the time) is a paradoxical instance of history looking forwards. Feminine sexual allure is represented in the play primarily by Mrs Chater, an Eve figure who has sex with four of the men and causes chaos. The gunshots heard at the closing of the scene are an interruption of the idyllic rural peacefulness and a reminder of the presence of death even, or especially, in Paradise — '*Et in Arcadia ego*'. There is something very pointed about Lady Croom using — and misusing — the Latin tag and addressing the threat of death, which will be fulfilled, to her daughter by name, at exactly the same time as recognising that the innocence of Eden has come to an end with the redesigning — and in her view ruining — of Sidley Park. Her observation that 'the guns have reached the brow' can be taken as another threat. Thomasina's response of 'phooey to Death!' is **hubris** and will be punished as such. Septimus, correcting the erroneous Latin translation of Lady Croom, also addresses a warning to Thomasina in his phrase 'A calendar of slaughter'. The scene ends with the prophetic and doom-laden stage direction: '*The guns are heard again, a little closer.*'

Act I scene 2

June, present day

Chloë welcomes the arrival of Bernard, who pretends to have come about the poet Ezra Chater, and goes to find Hannah, who is staying at Sidley Park while researching the history of the garden and its hermitage. Bernard has given a false name to disguise the fact that he is the unkind reviewer of Hannah's previous book on Lady Caroline Lamb, a mistress of Byron. Valentine passes through, looking for the commode that houses the game books. Hannah appears and discussion of the previous Croom family ensues. Hannah has discovered that Septimus's pupil was the Crooms's daughter, but does not know who the genius hermit was who left piles of papers behind that were found after his death. Bernard admits his real interest is Byron, not Chater, and produces the copy of *The Couch of Eros* found in Byron's library in 1816, containing the three letters we saw being put into it in the previous scene, which Bernard assumes concerned Byron himself and prove that Byron killed Chater in a duel and fled the country for that reason. We gather that Chloë fancies Bernard and that Gus has a crush on Hannah.

The plot and the connections between the characters of the two periods is established here. The scene begins in **farce genre**, with sudden entrances and exits and fortuitous timing, and ends in the same manner with Chloë interrupting a kiss between Bernard and Hannah, which could easily be misinterpreted, as indeed it is. Bernard is shown to be duplicitous and interested in fame and money. His assumed name of Peacock is relevant in various ways: as a bird image, as indicative of his vanity and flamboyant dress, and as the name of a Romantic **Gothic** novelist. Hannah's published work, *Caro*, is a link to the carnal theme (Latin '*caro, carnis*' (feminine) meaning 'flesh'). Similar linguistic playfulness is evident in Valentine's reference to the commode, which could mean a toilet or just a cupboard, and Bernard's misunderstanding is typical Stoppardian confusion and **comedy** on the linguistic, visual and situational levels. Although he mocks the stately home and its inhabitants by referring to them as 'Brideshead Regurgitated', Bernard is impressed by the set-up and enjoys rubbing shoulders with the aristocratic Coverlys. The fact that *The Couch of Eros* was rediscovered when a house was sold to make way for the Channel Tunnel rail-link supports Septimus's later claim that lost knowledge is always found again.

Act I scene 3

11 April 1809

Septimus reads another note from Chater and puts it in *The Couch of Eros*. He then writes a letter, seals it and puts it in his pocket. Thomasina is doing a Latin lesson, translating Plutarch. She is bored and annoyed with Septimus for teasing her, so suggests that her mother is sexually interested in Lord Byron — who is currently staying at Sidley Park — as a punishment for her husband, whose idea it is to landscape the park. This upsets Septimus, since he is himself sexually interested in Lady Croom. Thomasina mentions her maths insights into nature and numbers. Thomasina exits, annoyed that Septimus has translated Plutarch by using Shakespeare's version in ***Antony and Cleopatra***, which she regards as cheating, and Brice and Chater enter. The latter's confrontation with Septimus over insults to his wife and the now revealed authorship of the hostile review of *The Maid of Turkey* are interrupted by the entrance of Lady Croom, who insists that Byron must not be allowed to leave the house and that Septimus, his old schoolfriend, must do his bit to keep him there. She borrows Septimus's copy of *The Couch of*

Eros to lend to Byron, and instructs Septimus to 'take command' of Byron's pistols. A duel is agreed between Septimus and Chater for 5 a.m. the following morning behind the boathouse. Brice — whom Septimus accuses of having a relationship with Mrs Chater — is both Chater's second and the second duellist for Septimus to deal with.

The scene opening is a repeat of that of scene 1, with Septimus and Thomasina engaged in separate pursuits and Thomasina's telling Septimus that someone has been seen in the gazebo (this time Byron and Lady Croom). Triangular relationships — typically a cause of both comedy and **tragedy** — are highlighted in this scene; *Antony and Cleopatra* — a link between sex, literature and death — is a tragic triangular love story, whereas Thomasina's knowingness with regard to her mother's sexual indiscretions makes them amusing. It is significant, though apparently chance, that Thomasina chooses to use an apple leaf as the basis for her equations, given the symbolism of the apple in western literature. She continues to gain intellectual ascendancy over her tutor when she replies to his 'A fancy is not a discovery' that 'A gibe is not a rebuttal'. By having the last word she proves herself to be just as quick-thinking and actually cleverer than he is, and there is no doubt that she dominates the exchange on p. 49.

However, she makes a mis-prophecy when she tells Septimus that he 'will be famous for being my tutor when Lord Byron is dead and forgotten', though since she is a fictional character comparing another fictional character to a historical character, this is complicated in the extreme.

Septimus reassures Thomasina with his theory of recycled possessions and ideas, and in fact Thomasina's lesson book will not be lost when she is old. 'The procession is very long and life is very short' is an allusion to the Latin tag *ars longa, vita brevis*, which is normally interpreted pessimistically but which Septimus sees in a positive light. His belief that human history is cyclical not linear is destroyed by the Second Law of Thermodynamics and this explains why he takes it so badly to learn that 'we are all doomed'. 'Lord Byron was amusing at breakfast' is an ironic link back to p. 42 to prove Bernard wrong and set up the expectation that he always will be. 'I hope you die!' is a lighthearted and even amusing childish utterance on the one hand, but also an imminently rebounding death curse. Septimus, who *'has been watching Lady Croom's progress up the garden'* (though the audience cannot know this) suddenly changes to an irritable mood hitherto unsuspected in him, as if he is becoming less optimistic as the play progresses, or is suffering increasingly from the pangs of unrequited ardour.

Act I scene 4

June, present day

Hannah and Valentine are discussing Thomasina's maths primer and exercise book, found in Septimus's portfolio, and her work on the *New Geometry of Irregular Forms*. Valentine realises that she has been using iterated algorithms, which he finds incredible for her time. He is using the same methodology to study changes in the grouse population as a postgraduate biology research project. Bernard enters in a state of excitement, having just discovered the library copy of *English Bards and Scotch Reviewers* containing a superscription that he assumes is by Byron. Hannah presents Bernard with a letter from Lady to Lord Croom that proves that Chater was dead by 1810. Bernard lets his theorising run away with him, deducing that Chater must have challenged Byron to a duel over Mrs Chater and his reputation as a poet, and been killed. Hannah is sceptical, given that there is no evidence of how Chater died, and hitherto no proof that Byron ever visited Sidley Park. Valentine, however, says that he has come across Byron's name in the game book for 1809. Hannah remains more interested in Thomasina and her equations.

Another triangle emerges, that of the second Lady Croom, Chloë and Bernard. The discovery of three pieces of written evidence from long ago prove that things and knowledge are not permanently lost; 'It dropped from sight but we will write it again!' is Bernard echoing Septimus in the previous scene. On the other hand, discoveries are liable to be misconstrued by a later generation because of subjective interpretation or the data being incomplete, and therefore the cause of historical fallacies. Hannah takes the **Enlightenment** approach and Bernard the Romantic one, thus reversing normally perceived gender roles in relation to logic and fact versus imagination and fiction. Act I ends with a time jump to early the following morning and a pistol shot. This sound tricks the audience into believing that the duel took place and someone was indeed killed, showing how easily erroneous theories can be created from misleading evidence.

Act II scene 5

June, present day

Bernard is regaling Chloë, Gus and Valentine with the lecture on Byron the murderer, written for the Byron Society, when Hannah enters and disrupts him with questions of logic, which infuriates him. Chloë shows a partiality for Bernard by trying to help his argument. Valentine takes offence at Bernard's diatribe on the uselessness of science and storms out, followed by his siblings. Bernard also argues with Hannah about the sketch on the dust-jacket of *Caro*, which he claims is not really a picture of her with Byron. Bernard leaves for London after admitting to having had sex with Chloë and to his intention of returning for the dance as her date. Valentine comes back and gives Hannah the evidence (a letter containing his birth and death dates) which suggests that the hermit was Septimus.

The audience are expecting a Regency alternating scene according to the structure of the play so far. The fact that the pattern has now become unpredictable is a manifestation of the breakdown of order into chaos. Bernard is sex mad, like the focus of his literary endeavours, and even propositions Hannah, who is not interested. Valentine feeding the tortoise is a repetition of Septimus doing the same in scene 3.

Act II scene 6

12 April 1809

The following day, Jellaby receives Septimus back into the house at 5.30 a.m. with a rabbit he has shot for Thomasina. The duel did not take place. He tells Jellaby he spent the night in the boathouse and saw a carriage leaving the park in the early hours. He is informed that this contained Captain Brice and Mr and Mrs Chater, and that Byron left on horseback. They were all dismissed by Lady Croom after she discovered Mrs Chater coming out of Byron's room as she was on her way in. Lady Croom appears holding two letters written by Septimus — in case he was killed in the duel — to herself and Thomasina, which she has found in Septimus's room. Lady Croom threatens to dismiss Septimus as well, disapproving of the letters and of his relationship with Mrs Chater, but is diverted by Jellaby bringing in the tea tray and a letter from Byron addressed to Septimus, who sets fire to it unread. Lady Croom is placated by Septimus flattering her. We learn that the *ménage à trois* of the Chaters and Brice has gone to the West Indies, where her brother intends to set up Chater as a roving botanist. Lady Croom tells Septimus to come to her room at seven o'clock. Septimus burns the two farewell letters.

Scene 6 starts with a **reprise**. The dead rabbit with blood on it as a gift for Thomasina is another foreshadowing of her death; like the universe she is doomed. Shedding and picking up is illustrated by Septimus having Byron's pistols and Byron having Septimus's *The Couch of Eros*. The triangular relationships continue to be drawn attention to, with those involving Lady Croom, Thomasina, Septimus, Byron and Mrs Chater, Mr Chater and Captain Brice all referred to in this scene. Though a 'night of reckoning', sexual attraction cannot be reckoned and is the incalculable factor that, in Hannah's view in scene 5, is taking the world 'to hell in a handcart'. Although Lady Croom was anxious yesterday to keep Byron at Sidley Park, today she decreed his immediate departure. As Bernard said in the previous scene, 'Letters get lost'. That three letters are burned, one even before being read, draws attention to the randomness of the survival of documents and the inevitable gaps in evidence and knowledge.

Act II scene 7

3 June to 9 June 1812 and 9 June, present day

NB The two time periods are represented simultaneously and intermingled, but have been separated below to make the action easier to follow. Light changes signal the movement of time.

Present day in the morning

Gus, Valentine and Chloë are in Regency (1812) costume for a photograph to be taken prior to the annual fancy dress party ball. Chloë is reading about Bernard's theory in the Saturday papers. Valentine is continuing to work on Thomasina's

equations. Hannah enters with another newspaper. Chloë and Gus leave to sort out his costume. Valentine shows Hannah Thomasina's equations pushed through a computer. Hannah reveals that Thomasina died in a fire the night before her seventeenth birthday. She and Valentine intermittently discuss iteration and entropy.

June 1812. One week before Thomasina's seventeenth birthday

Septimus is reading Thomasina's maths book while Thomasina and Augustus are drawing geometrical solids. Thomasina admits to finding Byron attractive. Augustus complains that Byron claimed his hare. Septimus tries to get them to be quiet and offends Augustus, who leaves. Thomasina reveals that she has told Augustus that Septimus kissed her the day before in the hermitage (formerly the gazebo), and she insists on his teaching her to waltz. Septimus shows Thomasina a prize scientific essay that contradicts **determinism**. She says her mother is in love with the piano-tuning Count Zelinsky, who is playing in the next room until interfered with by Lady Croom, who enters complaining about the noise of the steam engine. She reveals her satisfaction in being 'the first in the kingdom to show a dahlia', thanks to her brother having married the widow of the botanist who discovered it, i.e. Mrs Chater. She asks Thomasina how old she is and realises it is time she were married. It turns out that she and Septimus (who were in London waltzing) and Count Zelinsky saw Byron the year before at the Royal Academy with Caroline Lamb, which proves Hannah is right and Bernard wrong about the Fuseli portrait. Lady Croom and Noakes discuss the need for a hermit. Thomasina gives Septimus a diagram of heat exchange and a drawing of himself with Plautus. Augustus reappears to ask Septimus to tell him the facts of life, having been told about 'carnal embrace' by Thomasina.

Present day in the afternoon

Chloë has been rounding up everyone for the photograph for the local paper. Bernard has arrived and is distressed to learn that he has been 'Fucked by a dahlia' when Hannah reveals from the garden books that Chater died in Martinique of a monkey bite (and therefore was not killed by Byron in a duel at Sidley Park) and that she has written to *The Times* to say so. Bernard, who has been to London to give his talk and appear on 'The Breakfast Hour', dresses up for the photo but hides his face.

June 1812. The eve of Thomasina's seventeenth birthday

Septimus is studying Thomasina's diagram by the light of an oil lamp when she enters in her nightgown with a candlestick. She wants to waltz but Septimus orders her to be silent and wait for appropriate music while he reads her essay. He realises that the 'Improved Newtonian Universe must cease and grow cold'. Septimus and Thomasina kiss and dance.

Present day in the evening

Valentine and Hannah enter from the party and study Thomasina's diagram. Bernard enters at a run and says his goodbyes. He has been caught by Lady Croom in the hermitage with Chloë.

Finale

Septimus lights Thomasina's candlestick and warns her to 'Be careful with the flame'. They waltz once more, for her birthday. Gus gives Hannah a folio containing Thomasina's drawing of Septimus holding Plautus, and he invites her to dance. Both couples waltz to the piano music.

Time unrolls to create patterns. This scene is an overlay of new over old, or old over new, like a landscape design book. The piano and steam engine compete noisily; the music of the two periods fuse, with modern sound from the marquee segueing into Count Zelinsky's playing of waltzes on the piano. Events, actions and speeches are 'doubled by time'; Lady Croom's complaint to Noakes is a reprise of her objections in the first scene to his designs on her garden, proving her prophecy to have come true; Augustus walking out in a huff repeats the action of Valentine when patronised by Bernard; Chloë discusses determinism with Valentine just as Thomasina did with Septimus in the first scene, and repeats Thomasina's view that the future is all programmed, except for 'people fancying people who aren't supposed to be in that part of the plan'; the extract from Byron's poem 'Darkness' (1816) is a description of the world going cold, 'Rayless, and pathless', 'blind and blackening', which is both a chilling futuristic vision and a meeting of poetry and physics, art and science. (It actually refers to the lost summer of 1816 when a colossal volcanic explosion in Indonesia caused snow in New England in August, an excellent example of Chaos Theory.) We also see characteristics duplicated, e.g. Thomasina shows a passion for fashion and fear of being 'despised', which is reminiscent of her mother, and the modern Lady Croom, in fancying Bernard, is continuing the proclivities of her former namesake.

We are not surprised to discover that Gus enjoys dressing up, as he belongs to the past era and his attraction to Hannah is based on her genuine desire to discover more about it. They are whisked back into the Regency period to join Septimus and Thomasina, their idols, at the end.

Bernard's last utterance, the challenging imperative 'Publish!', is an allusion to 'Publish and be damned!' apparently said by the Duke of Wellington to the courtesan Harriet Wilson when she threatened to expose him by publishing her memoirs. Like the beating of a butterfly's wings, a small random event — where Thomasina places her candle — will have huge consequences: her premature death, the madness and early death of Septimus, the loss of her mathematical genius for nearly 200 years, the direction taken by the Coverly family that can generate only through Augustus. The time jump of a week in 1812 at p. 122 — though it is manifestly a continuation of the same party day in the present — is perplexing. On p. 112 Thomasina states very exactly that she is 16 years 11 months and three weeks old, yet Hannah tells Valentine on p. 101 that she died 'The night before her seventeenth birthday'. Perhaps Stoppard is proving Bernard's point that 'Everything moved more slowly then' (p. 78), i.e. a present day contains as much action as a week in 1809. What is clear is that Thomasina and Septimus represent the Romantic imagination and to prove Hannah's thesis of its 'breakdown' they must both die (as do Byron and Lady Caroline Lamb) before the end of the period, the death of Coleridge in 1834.

Ending with a dance, a fusion of science (predetermined steps in a fixed pattern) and art (aesthetic performance involving senses and feeling) is a suitable joint icon as well as a romantic celebratory union. If the world is doomed, one might as well dance. It is 'A dance to the music of time' (the legend to a Poussin painting of nymphs). Though associated with the resolution of comedy endings, as in Shakespeare, it also points up the tragedy to follow immediately afterwards, that Thomasina and Septimus's budding relationship is doomed to last only one evening. Thomasina's claim that 'we have time' gives **pathos** and dramatic **irony** to the ending. The other dancing couple brings the two halves of the play together — and the 'four people the play loves' (Barton) — satisfactorily in harmony and symmetry, reminding us that some things do not change, and dancing in pairs as an expression of love is one of them.

Dramatis personae

There are two groups of characters in *Arcadia*, who share a location but inhabit different time zones: Regency and the present day (which was actually 1993 when the play was first performed). The two groups mirror each other across the time gap; as well as sharing the same set and props, they have similar interests and are on a quest for similar answers. They appear together, though are unaware of each other, in the last scene.

Regency period

Septimus Hodge

Aged 22, Septimus Hodge is tutor (and later more) to Thomasina, an admirer of Lady Croom, and he also has sexual encounters with Mrs Chater, a visitor to Sidley Park. He studied maths and natural philosophy at Trinity College, Cambridge, where he was a contemporary of Byron, who was also a schoolfriend at Harrow. He is both a linguist and a scientist, currently teaching Thomasina maths and Latin and, at the end, how to waltz. He becomes the hermit of Sidley Park, having apparently gone insane as a result of either his pupil's discovery of the doomed universe or her tragic death, and spends the next 20 years, until his own death in 1834, living in the hermitage and doing maths equations. His brother is editor of the literary magazine called the *Piccadilly Recreation*, a 'thrice weekly folio sheet' for which Septimus writes book reviews. He is competitive and without modesty: 'At Harrow I was better at this than Lord Byron' (p. 51). Though generally urbane, unsentimental (he says sex is nicer than love) and with sarcasm as his weapon, he is nonetheless capable of passion and of losing his temper; he does not tolerate fools, such as Brice and Chater, gladly. His name in Latin means 'seventh', which would suggest that he has more than one elder sibling. Hodge was the name of Dr Johnson's cat.

Thomasina Coverly

Nearly 14, like Shakespeare's Juliet, she is intense, spirited and precocious; Stoppard calls her 'mercurial'. Her first question in the opening line of the play suggests that she has just arrived at an important coming-of-age point in her life: an interest in sex. Her drawing of a heat engine proves that she anticipated the Second Law of Thermodynamics. She dies in a fire on the eve of her seventeenth birthday. As well as being based on Byron's mathematical prodigy of a daughter, Ada Lovelace, she could be seen as a fictional precursor of the inquisitive and irrepressible Victorian female child, Alice, created by the Oxford mathematics don Charles Dodgson. Her delight at the prospect of rice pudding with jam shows that she still has traits of childhood in 1809, but by 1812 her mind is on more adult things, such as fashions and relationships. It is a 'diabolically difficult' part for any actress to encompass as a whole.

Augustus Coverly

Aged 15 in 1809, Thomasina's elder brother is at Eton. He apparently shoots a hare which is claimed as his own shot by Byron. His only other contribution to the plot is to ask Septimus to tell him the facts of life at the end of the play, thus bringing it around in a circle to the beginning, when Thomasina wants Septimus to impart to her the same knowledge of carnal matters. His Roman emperor name is synonymous with the Age of Reason, and was that of one of George III's sons.

Lady Croom

Mother of Augustus and Thomasina, Lady Croom is the *grande dame* of Sidley Park, who has sexual designs on a Polish pianist, her distant aristocratic neighbour Lord Byron and her daughter's tutor. She married at 17 and now, in her mid-thirties, she is bored with her inadequate husband and jealous of rivals, including her daughter. Somewhat negligent as a mother, she affects not to know Thomasina's age, and fears that she is being over-educated for marriage. Like Lady Bracknell in Oscar Wilde's *The Importance of Being Earnest*, she is anti-intellectual, domineering and censorious ('I cannot approve' p. 96) and speaks in epigrams. She wishes above all things to be fashionable — hence her interest in the wearing of drawers and her pride in being 'the first in the kingdom to show a dahlia'. She expels Mrs Chater, Mr Chater, her brother Captain Brice and Lord Byron in the middle of the night, after discovering the former leaving Byron's room, where she herself was heading. Her belief that she is always right — though she is often wrong, as when insisting that a rabbit is a hare — and her readiness to lie is symptomatic of the play's problem of being able to ascertain the truth about anything. She also lends credence to the theory of the unpredictability and unaccountability of sexual attraction, the 'defect of God's humour' (p. 95).

Ezra Chater

According to Septimus, who reviews them, Chater's poetic works — *The Maid of Turkey* and *The Couch of Eros* — are without any merit other than a soporific one. He is a guest at Sidley Park only because Captain Brice invites him there in order to have access to his wife. Chater goes as a botanist to the West Indies, where he dies in 1810 at the age of 32 from a monkey bite. He is very stupid and no match for Septimus, who has cuckolded him; nor is he aware that Captain Brice is his wife's long-term lover.

Captain Edward Brice

Lady Croom's brother is a naval officer who brings the Chaters to Sidley Park, and then takes them with him to the West Indies on his ship in order for Mr Chater to be kept engaged in botanical research while he enjoys Mrs Chater. It turns out that he also paid 50 pounds to have Chater published, in order to keep him compliant. His readiness to act as Chater's second for a duel with Septimus may be influenced by the convenience to himself if Chater were to be killed. After the death of Mr Chater in Martinique a year later, he marries Mrs Chater. He shares his sister's conservative views on landscape gardening and Thomasina's education, and also her tendency to talk epigrammatically, though in his case it is merely 'fortuitous wit'.

Richard Noakes

A middle-aged landscape architect ('landskip gardener') hired by Lord Croom, he is 'a philosopher of the picturesque', 'The Emperor of Irregularity', tasked with re-modelling the garden in the latest style. With his 'before and after' sketch book he represents the historical figure, Humphry Repton. His role is that of the serpent in the garden, a bringer of noise and chaos that destroys the previous Eden-like perfection of Sidley Park. Lady Croom calls him the horticultural equivalent of a bull in a china shop. Because he informs Chater of the tryst between Septimus and Mrs Chater in the gazebo (which is overheard by the groom who tells Jellaby), he is the spy (with his theodolite) who introduces unwelcome knowledge and shatters the harmonious relations at Sidley Park at the start of the play. Septimus, who considers him to be no better than 'a jumped-up jobbing gardener', calls him a 'muddy-mettled rascal', a disparaging quotation from *Hamlet* that Noakes is not well enough educated to recognise. He is insensitive, obtuse and constantly baffled by the conversation of the other characters.

Jellaby

Jellaby is a stereotypical middle-aged butler who owes something of his knowing-ness and superciliousness to the butler Lane in *The Importance of Being Earnest*. He performs a practical plot function in bringing in letters and information at opportune moments, and in generally representing the otherwise invisible servant class who notice and gossip about the loose behaviour of their supposed superiors. He has a comical Dickensian name.

Present day

The Coverlys are an old Norman aristocratic family, the de Coverlys. They gave their name to an English country dance connected to fox-hunting.

Valentine Coverly

The romantically named Valentine is a postgraduate mathematician at Oxford in his late twenties, and future Earl of Croom. Using 200 years' worth of Sidley Park game books (in which the game killed by shooting parties is recorded and attributed) he is charting changes in the grouse population, linking science to nature by trying to formulate a model using a computer. He pretends to be Hannah's fiancé as a joke. He is initially sceptical about the possibility of Thomasina having discovered iterative algorithms as early as 1812. He is disparagingly described by Bernard as 'Brideshead Regurgitated'.

Chloë Coverly

The bossy 18-year-old daughter of the house takes a fancy to Bernard, presumably because he is the only available non-relative male. She flirts with him throughout in a way that reminds us of Mrs Chater's promiscuous behaviour, and is also reminiscent of Thomasina's crush on her tutor. There are other parallels with Thomasina in her temperament and in some of her questions and comments. She is caught *in flagrante* with Bernard in the hermitage by her mother, but is unrepentant.

Gus Coverly

The present-day namesake of Augustus is played by the same actor, and can even wear the same costume in the final scene. For reasons never explained, the mute, autistic, Gus stopped speaking at the age of five, but he is an intelligent presence, a damaged Romantic figure who seems to belong to the past and has intuitive under-standing of what happened in it. He 'loves going through' old stuff. He is fond of Hannah, presumably because of her interest in the house, garden and former inhab-itants of Sidley Park. Since Thomasina died, and the Coverly name is still going strong, Gus must be in direct lineal descent from the Regency Augustus who wanted to know about procreation.

Hannah Jarvis

An author in her late thirties, Hannah wrote *Caro*, a biography of Lady Caroline Lamb, which was given a hostile review by Bernard. She is 'doing landscape and literature 1750 to 1834' and staying at the house in order to do research. She had previously sent a copy of *Caro* to Lady Croom, since Caroline Lamb had a fine garden, and was invited by 'Hermione' to write a history of the Sidley Park garden. While trying to solve the mystery of the identity of the hermit of Sidley Park, she discovers a lesson book that contains Thomasina's experiments with iterative functions. She does not jump to conclusions and represents a rationalist worldview; 'She wears nothing frivolous'. She would seem to have feminist sympathies, given her lack of interest in men (she calls them 'you people') and her choice of book subject (a victim of Byron's philandering), and to be unfeminine to the extent that she does not care about her appearance and might smoke '*brown-paper cigarillos*'. According to Valentine, 'She won't let anyone kiss her' and she does not like dancing. Persistent rather than brilliant (she is '*not quick enough*' on p. 35), she is the tortoise who wins the race against Bernard the hare and has the last laugh on the letters page of *The Times*. She also has the last word in the play. Hannah seems to owe something to the prickly literary sleuth Maud Bailey in A. S. Byatt's novel *Possession*.

Bernard Nightingale

A literature don at Sussex University, in his late thirties, Bernard is 'on the make' for both sex and fame as a critic. He is a media don who engages in performance art. He comes to Sidley Park to search for evidence that Byron visited there, though he at first pretends to be on a different quest and agrees to give a false name to deceive Hannah into not realising that he is the same person who harshly reviewed her book on Lady Caroline Lamb. He creates a theory to suit his ambition, regardless of facts, which leads him to the erroneous conviction that Byron was forced to disappear abroad in 1809 because he had killed his fellow poet Chater in a duel at Sidley Park. He stays overnight at a pub in the local village and returns next day to practise the speech he goes to London with to give to the Byron Society. He returns for the party to partner Chloë and is expelled from the house by Lady Croom after being caught with Chloë in the hermitage, which reprises the events in 1809 of Septimus meeting Mrs Chater in the same location for the same purpose, and of Byron and Mrs Chater being expelled for the same reason by the earlier Lady Croom.

Hannah calls him 'arrogant, greedy and reckless', which are not the qualities one would expect in a scholar. He resents the fame, status and money that scientists are given and is tactless and combative in discourse with others. His surname links him wittily to romance and the Romantics, as well as to the play's running bird gag. As Chloë points out, he is ostentatious and 'not really a Nightingale', as his '*peacock-coloured display handkerchief*' and his red Mazda indicate. His name is strikingly similar to that of Benedict Nightingale, *The Times* theatre critic who has reviewed most of Stoppard's plays over the last few decades and who describes Bernard in his review of this play as a 'predatory popinjay'. The part was written for the actor Bill Nighy, whose name may also have influenced Stoppard's choice, as might that of the poet Nightshade, a character in Peacock's satirical **Gothic** novel *Headlong Hall.*

Missing characters

The play contains characters who are referred to and who are important to the plot, but who never appear on stage. It is worth considering their role and the reasons why the audience are not allowed to meet them:

- **Byron:** he is a non-fictional character in a fictional play, and the mysterious blank at the centre of the action around whom the other characters revolve.
- **Mrs Chater:** it is not necessary to see her as the audience are given a full picture of her behaviour through the other characters' comments; Lady Croom calls her a 'trollop' and 'the village noticeboard'. She is a sexual force, a garden **nymph** who represents Eve and is the cause of the expulsion from Paradise of herself, her husband, her future husband and Lord Byron — and very nearly of Septimus. The name suggests an amalgam of chaser and cheater. Her first name, Charity, is ironic (she is very generous with herself) and ambiguous ('deny it for Charity's sake'). It is given by her new husband to the dwarf dahlia discovered by her previous husband, which becomes a proud possession of Lady Croom. Practically speaking, she does not appear because during the one day she remains at Sidley Park she feels it advisable to 'keep her room'.
- **Lady Croom (2):** a lurking, snooping presence, she reprises not only the name but the role of her predecessor when she discovers Chloë in the hermitage with Bernard and causes him to leave suddenly and in disgrace. (She is also a second Noakes, associated with the spying tool, the theodolite.) The audience see a mental reincarnation of, and hears the voice of, the Regency Lady Croom when the modern one is referred to, so it is as if she has time-jumped to the present and nothing has changed. Like her ancestor, Hermione is an imperious character, and not a great reader (except for her gardening books), who seeks to impress in wanting to be known for her garden.
- **Lord Croom (1):** it adds to his humorous ineffectualness that he has no stage presence (like Lord Bracknell who is absent from Wilde's play) and is conveniently deaf. His voice is heard in the game book as 'self'. His interest in life seems to be death, i.e. the killing of wildlife.
- There is also an absent present-day **Lord Croom (2):** we know he dislikes typewriters, homosexuals and Japanese cars. We could infer that he is a 'dinosaur' eccentric living in a time warp rejecting all new inventions and ideas, were it not that he reads tabloid newspapers.

- **Zelinsky** plays the piano in an adjacent room on more than one occasion but we see him only through the eyes of Lady Croom and Septimus, as either a Polish count or a piano tuner respectively. He provides comedy in this ambiguous role and as the cause of Septimus's jealousy. One gets the impression that there have been many, and will be more, exotic foreign artistes in Lady Croom's life.
- **The garden** is central to the play and gives it its title; it is the reason for all the external entrances and exits, but is tantalisingly invisible. It is a space to be filled in a play about the filling of spaces, the putting in of the missing notes until the tune is distinguishable.

Character types and relationships

Triangular relationships

There are a striking number of three-way actual or would-be romantic/sexual relationships in the play:

- Lady Croom (1) and Thomasina and Septimus
- Lady Croom (1) and Mrs Chater and Septimus
- Lady Croom (1) and Mrs Chater and Byron
- Lady Croom (1) and Septimus and Byron
- Lady Croom (1) and Septimus and Count Zelinsky
- Hannah and Chloë and Bernard
- Hannah and Gus and Valentine
- Brice and Mrs Chater and Mr Chater
- Bernard and Chloë and Lady Croom (2)

Eternal triangles are tragic if love is involved, but comic if it is not. Marital or parental love is entirely absent from the play, making love of ideas, rather than people, the main emotional focus.

Names and titles

Characters reveal their own and others' status and their feelings towards each other by their choice of address. Septimus always calls Thomasina 'my lady', and Lady Croom 'madam' or 'your ladyship' though the former, surprisingly, calls him 'Septimus' and the latter calls him 'Mr Hodge'. Thomasina shows little reverence for any adult, including her mother, whom she calls 'mama' but without any affection. Byron is accorded his title of 'Lord', except by Thomasina, who is corrected by Septimus for not doing so. Mrs Chater is always thus called, even by her husband, which, although normal for the time, takes on an ironic nuance in the circumstances. The four other visitors generally call each other by their surnames — Hodge, Chater, Brice and Noakes — which reminds us of the rivalry or lack of approval that exists between them, as otherwise a 'Mr' or 'Captain' would have been appended to show respect. They call Lady Croom 'your ladyship'; even her own brother calls Lady Croom by her title, and we are never told her first name. Jellaby does not have one either, because in those days butlers were summoned by their surname, and their first name was probably not even known by the family. Gus must be a short form of Augustus, which is never used for him, whereas conversely his ancestor's name is not shortened to Gus. Obviously relationships have become less formal, and the class hierarchy less enforced, by the modern period, where the characters move swiftly to first names. Even so, Bernard is struck by the familiarity with which Hannah calls Lady Croom (2) 'Hermione', which suggests her lack of awe of the aristocracy.

Rational and romantic characters

Some characters are associated with thinking, some with feeling, and some cross the divide. Although **Romanticism** is most closely associated with the arts as the expression of aesthetic sensibility and talent, the movement also dabbled in the sciences insofar as they related to divine and human powers, the secrets of the universe and the occult, Mary Shelley's *Frankenstein* (1818) being an example.

Hannah is a Classicist and sees the garden changes as a 'decline from thinking to feeling' and a victim of 'Romantic sham', 'cheap thrills and false emotion'. Valentine refers to her '**classical** reserve' (p. 99). Bernard tells Hannah 'It takes a romantic to make a heroine of Caroline Lamb. You were cut out for Byron' (p. 84).

Valentine is a committed scientist and has no time for the arts as such. 'What matters is the calculus. Scientific progress. Knowledge' (p. 80). However, Hannah thinks he is a biologist (though he is actually a mathematician) because of his grouse research, and he crosses the divide in that respect, as his computer analysis is fed by nature and family history. He is also Romantic by temperament in that he is fascinated by the unknown ('these things are full of mystery', p. 62), passionate about the joy of being alive at a time when discoveries are being made, and given to venting annoyance and showing frustration with his work.

Bernard is actually a Romantic because he lacks clear-headedness and discretion and follows his gut feelings, his 'visceral belief', despite professing admiration for Byron because he 'was an eighteenth-century Rationalist'. This leads him, along with his male chauvinism, to think that Caroline Lamb 'was Romantic waffle on wheels with no talent' (p. 79).

Gus is romantic because he dresses the part, has suffered a mysterious trauma and behaves entirely intuitively.

Captain Brice has no illusions about mistress Chater but 'would die for her'. His role is parodically reminiscent of that of Lancelot, who loved Guinevere and deceived her husband, King Arthur.

Septimus develops from a stereotypically urbane Augustan figure, restrained and dispassionate, with the demeanour and speech characteristics of a rationalist and satirist, to a reflective, sensitive, introverted one, finally dying as that most extreme of Romantic figures, the emaciated mad hermit living in a wilderness. He represents the Romantic imagination in becoming a recluse with only a tortoise for company, and his death coincides with the death of Coleridge and that of the movement. His change mirrors that of the garden.

Thomasina approves of the picturesque 'improvements' ('In my opinion Mr Noakes's scheme for the garden is perfect', p. 14) and wants to marry Lord Byron, as well as learn to waltz and follow fashions. Her Romantic desires to dance and to seduce her tutor are a prelude to her sensational death. She is also demonstratively emotional and unconventional, although her mathematical rigour and determination to succeed are traits of a disciplined and rational mind.

Paired characters

Some characters are similar enough in personality, interests, relationships, situations, events or fates to be linked across the two time periods.

The two Lord Crooms, Lady Crooms and Augustus/Gus are obviously meant to be paired. Gus inherits Thomasina's role of teenage prodigy, showing intuitive understanding and baffling his elders. His giving Hannah an apple plus leaf suggests he wants her to discover Thomasina's important work with fractals.

Hannah and Thomasina are both independent females capable of lateral thinking and seeing the truth that others deny and ridicule. They both make discoveries with an apple leaf.

Septimus and Bernard are both literary reviewers/scholars; both are womanisers and pursue the daughters of the house; both are fancied by the mothers/Lady Crooms; both are competitive and with a high opinion of themselves.

Hannah and Lady Croom (1) value order and harmony, as represented by the natural landscaping of Capability Brown, and lament the destruction of the garden.

Thomasina and Chloë are the teenage daughters of their respective families who have grown out of childish pleasures and have designs on educated men. Chloë's rampant sexuality and garden assignation also connect her to Mrs Chater.

Septimus and Gus are both, ultimately, recluses, the spirits that haunt Sidley Park.

Bernard and Ezra Chater both want to believe in something so much that they confuse their desire for it to be so with proof that it is so.

Sympathetic characters

Stoppard has been accused by critics of not creating characters an audience can care about, of using them only as vehicles for **repartee**. However, the critic Anne Barton assumes that her readers all agree when she refers to the 'Four loved characters', i.e. Septimus, Thomasina, Hannah and Gus. The audience cannot love characters they do not care about, and they cannot care about characters who have not engaged them intellectually or emotionally, or both. These four characters are sympathetic because of their humanity, innocence, wit or compassion — or some

093974

Student Text Guide

combination of these qualities — and they elicit admiration at the end of the play because of both who they are and what they have achieved, as well as concern for what is going to happen to them in the future. They do, indeed, produce an amusing line in repartee, but so does Bernard, and we really do not care what happens to him, as he actually invites and deserves his comeuppance. The other characters do not engage us because they are silly or stereotypical or apparently devoid of real feeling, with the possible exception of Valentine. He, like the beloved four, is capable of love, not just lust or infatuation, at least with regard to his work.

Tortoise shells

A critic has described the main characters of the play as having carapaces behind which they hide to protect their true selves. Septimus gives the impression of being the urbane wit, always ready with a ***bon mot*** and without feelings of any kind, but there is a tenderness in his treatment of Thomasina (bringing her a rabbit for a pie, agreeing to dance with her) that belies the apparent cool indifference. His becoming the hermit suggests that his inner self breaks out of its restraint as a result of grief at her death.

Thomasina's switches from comic to serious are a paradigm for the play, but they also disguise her depth of feeling on any matter. Her uncompromising regard for the truth is veiled by her playful tone and her trivial references to food, animals and fashions, so that only belatedly do the audience, and Septimus, realise that she is a genius who could change the world. The social disapproval of cleverness in young women is revealed by Lady Croom and her brother, who are afraid that Thomasina will not be able to marry — a fate worse than death — if she is too serious and knowledgeable. Even Septimus warns her 'You must not be cleverer than your elders. It is not polite'. This attitude explains her need to adopt a flippancy that belies her intellect.

The present-day characters do not seem to need to hide their thoughts and feelings and needs, which may be a comment on the change of codes of behaviour over the centuries, whereby nowadays one dare be open and individual in a way that Regency people dared not, for fear of censure and social ostracism ('comment on the platform', as Lady Bracknell calls it). Hannah is wedded to her work and also likely to remain unmarried; the stigma has gone, but Chloë still tries to matchmake for her. Though generally assertive, Hannah has moments of self-doubt, as revealed in her sudden admission that she knows 'Nothing'. Bernard does not have the self- or social awareness to see that he should rein himself in and control his behaviour and expression if he wishes to be respected in the academic and publishing world, or to understand that he is not God's gift to women. Apart from his seeming impressed by the social rank of the Coverlys, there is no evidence that he is hiding a less confident and less objectionable persona within, although he is capable of being moved by poetry.

Plot, structure and time

The structure of *Arcadia* is unusual: it consists of, in effect, two parallel plays that take place in the same room but 180 years apart. Some of the characters in the 1993 scenes are directly descended from characters in the 1809/1812 scenes; others have counterparts in the earlier period. In the long final scene, the two separate plays merge; both sets of characters are on stage simultaneously, sharing the same props and wearing similar costumes, and although each group is acting out its own independent script, the dialogues overlap and often appear to be sequential. The language, topics and characters of the two periods are neatly combined, like jam in rice.

At nearly three hours, *Arcadia* is unusually long for a modern play. It is divided into seven scenes of unequal length that are set as follows: 1809, 1993, 1809, 1993, 1993, 1809, 1812 and 1993. The regular alternation of period scenes in Act I creates the impression that this pattern will continue throughout the play, but it breaks down between the Acts. This example of the breakdown of formal structure is a paradigm of the intrusion of chaos into a predetermined and regular order, which is one of the things the play is about.

April 1809 and June 1812

The play is firmly rooted in its historical context: this period was an important turning point in garden design, it was the culmination of the clash between the **Enlightenment** and **Romanticism**, and it was the time when new botanical species were being imported into England from voyages of discovery. The obvious answer to 'Why 1809?' is that for three days in April of that year Byron's whereabouts were, and still are, as a matter of historical fact, unknown; what *is* known is that he left the country shortly afterwards, and he could, therefore, have gone to the equivalent of Sidley Park during those days and had an experience there to explain his need to flee. Byron has been claimed for both sides, by the rationalists and the Romantics, so his mysterious movements in the spring of that year are of great interest to literary academics. In addition, some critics have seen parallels between this play and Goethe's novel *Elective Affinities* (*Die Wahlverwandtschaften*), which is based on the principle of chemical attractions and was published in 1809.

The final scene has to be set in 1812 so that it takes place after Byron's return from Europe in 1811 and after his affair with Caroline Lamb. It is also the year in which important work on thermodynamics was happening in Paris. The three-year time jump shows Thomasina's development from a precocious child to a young adult on the brink of a future as a mathematician and as a woman.

Extra-textual events

There are historical or fictional events that occur before, after and during the time frame of the Regency play, which are relevant to what happens in it:

1687	publication of Newton's *Principia*
1787	birth of Septimus
1788	birth of Byron
1795	birth of Thomasina on 10 June
1808	Chater writes *The Maid of Turkey*, reviewed by Septimus in the *Piccadilly Recreation*
1809	Chater writes *The Couch of Eros*, sent to Septimus at Sidley Park to be reviewed
1809	Byron writes to his lawyer on 16 April, announcing his intention to leave England
1809	Septimus's review of *The Couch of Eros* published on 30 April
1811	Joseph Fourier's prize essay published
1812	death of Thomasina on 10 June
1816	Byron leaves England for good and his books are sold
1822	Joseph Fourier publishes *Théorie Analytique de la Chaleur*
1824	death of Byron in Greece. His body is returned, paraded in London, and buried at Newstead Abbey
1824	Sadi Carnot publishes account of heat engines, precursor to Second Law of Thermodynamics
1828	death of Lady Caroline Lamb
1832	*The Peak Traveller and Gazetteer* refers to the Sidley Park hermit
1834	Septimus, alias the hermit, dies aged 47; death of Coleridge
1859	Darwin's *The Origin of Species* published
1862	*Cornhill Magazine* quotes Peacock's letter to Thackeray in an essay on hermits

Merging of plots

The two plots relate to each other intimately from start to finish, and it is therefore fitting that they should merge in the final scene. The audience have the unique experience of seeing, in parallel, what actually happened during the key three days in 1809 and the attempts to reconstruct them by Bernard and Hannah during a few days in 1993. This is both a satisfying yet unsettling experience for the audience; it also throws important light on the process of scholarship, the incompleteness of surviving evidence, and what it is legitimate to infer from limited sources. Some of the conclusions of the twentieth-century scholars, we can see, are true, although as often from guesswork as from solid evidence; and others, particularly Bernard's unfounded assumption that Byron fought a duel with Chater, spectacularly wrong. The modern characters seem to become increasingly immersed in the past they are reconstructing, and it therefore seems natural for them to become part of it, to the extent that in scene 7 the same item is being inspected in both time periods simultaneously: on p. 103 Hannah is looking through Thomasina's lesson book at the same time as Septimus is examining it, and this idea is repeated on p. 124, where

'*Septimus and Valentine study the diagram doubled by time*'. The interleaving of the 1812 and 1993 scenes repeatedly gives rise to **juxtapositions** of utterances. Some create *double entendres* or comic effects, while others emphasise the interrelatedness of the two strands, e.g. on p. 105 where Hannah concludes 'Byron' and Thomasina virtually echoes her.

The fact that the final scene takes place three years later than the previous scenes shows Thomasina's progression from innocence to experience, from asking about to participating in carnal embrace, and also her maturing confidence in her mathematical skills. The convergence of the plots gives the audience the impression that matters are moving towards a conclusion (which they are, but it is an unpredictable one). The ultimate scene of the fire, which explains some of the mysteries that the twentieth-century characters have been trying to unravel, is withheld, leaving more questions frustratingly unanswered for the latter-day sleuths and for the audience. The finale has music, mathematics and 'the attraction which Newton left out' (p. 97); Thomasina now has 'a carcass of her own' (p. 15), and a pleasing circularity and fulfilment of prophecy have been achieved. In the twentieth century, it is Gus who invites Hannah to dance, as if they are the latter-day counterparts of the doomed lovers, and Thomasina's drawing of Septimus and Plautus, one of the strongest links between the two plots, is the last item discovered. The audience are made to feel privileged to have seen the 'real' Thomasina and Septimus, but this also makes their respective death and decline more poignant for us than it can be for Hannah, for all her sympathy. It underlines the power of perspective in influencing emotional reactions.

Layers

As with archaeology, the play is layered, and it also sees history as layers, so it is appropriate that this should be visually represented. The props are allowed to accumulate on stage to represent this idea that the past is only temporarily buried and will be rediscovered. Romanticism imposed itself on the Enlightenment, but the latter is still there — as illustrated by the modern characters dressing up as their Regency counterparts — just as the modern period is built on the stratum of Romanticism. Shedding, burying, digging, re-emerging and discovering are all actions that are the cause and effect of layering; they are explored both actually and metaphorically throughout the play, e.g. the physical excavation of the garden is paralleled by the digging for evidence in the library. Characters in both periods read from texts that were written before their own time, but also after in the case of the Regency period. That Gus is as physically indistinguishable from Augustus (being the same actor) as the two tortoises are (being the same tortoise) reminds the audience of how time can in fact go backwards as well as forwards. The garden indelibly preserves the imprint of its own historical phases; Capability Brown's boathouse still has foundations below the earth.

Teasing the audience

Stoppard uses the movements between the two time frames to manipulate or mislead the audience. The apple (itself a highly charged symbol in the play) appears in scene 2 and is given to Hannah by Gus (p. 45), but it is then eaten by Septimus and Plautus (p. 47) — 180 years earlier. This both emphasises the connection between the two periods (and is a prophetic preview of scene 7) and is an example of reverse temporal causation. It is a double bluff on the audience to make us think there was no hermit that we see Thomasina draw one in as a joke. We also assume, wrongly, that Plautus the tortoise is an amusing prop with no serious role, but discover at the very end that it is the crucial evidence to prove Hannah's theory of the identity of the Sidley Park hermit.

Scene 4 (1993) ends with early morning and a pistol shot — a transition to the next scene — which, after the Act interval, is in fact 1993 again; but it is echoed at the beginning of scene 6 (1809) where Stoppard describes the pistol shot and the crows as '*a reprise*'. It is misleading each time, because on neither occasion was a duel fought, it turns out. This is an example of reversing the usual process of **drama**: characters usually learn with or before the audience; here, they repeatedly learn later. A further example of playing with the time frame is that the third letter found in Septimus's portfolio (on p. 41) has not 'yet' been delivered — Septimus receives it on p. 46. This is one of many examples of reverse cause and effect, whereby the 1993 characters find, refer to or speculate about something 'before', in play time, it has happened in the earlier time-line — which disproves the 'Time's Arrow' thesis in the play.

Written evidence

The 1993 characters attempt to reconstruct the events of the nineteenth century by referring to the available documents, listed in the table below.

Written evidence	Page	What happens to it
The Couch of Eros	1	Lady Croom gives to Byron; Byron's library
Thomasina's maths primer (belonging to Septimus)	1	Septimus's portfolio (p. 56)
Letter 1: Chater's summons to Septimus to a duel	5	In *The Couch of Eros* (p. 41)
Dedication by Chater to Septimus	12	In fly-leaf of *The Couch of Eros*
Noakes's sketch book	13	Sidley Park library
Letter 2: Mrs Chater's note to Septimus	18	In *The Couch of Eros* (p. 41)
Thomasina's sketch of hermit in Noakes's book	18	Sidley Park library

Written evidence	Page	What happens to it
Game books referring to number of birds shot	23	Found in commode, by Valentine?
Hannah's book *Caro*	(24)	—
Catalogue of the Sidley Park library	(32)	Sidley Park library
Essay on hermits, *Cornhill Magazine*	34	(A library)
Letter to *Cornhill Magazine* by Peacock	(35)	(East India Library, Blackfriars) (p. 71)
Hundreds of pages of hermit's papers (calculations)	(37)	All burned after hermit's death
Engraving of Sidley Park in 1730	(36)	Sidley Park library
Lady Croom's garden books	38	Sidley Park library (p. 100)
Letter 3: Chater to Septimus	41	In *The Couch of Eros* (p. 41) and (p. 46)
Thomasina's lesson book	48	Septimus's portfolio (p. 56)
Letter from Septimus (*The Couch of Eros* review)	49	(Posted)
English Bards and Scotch Reviewers (annotated)	64	Sidley Park library
Letter from Lady to Lord Croom (re Brice's marriage)	64	Sidley Park library?
Byron Society Journal	83	—
Fuseli study in ink of Byron and Caro	(83)	(A gallery)
Peaks Traveller extract of 1832	85	(A library)
Septimus's letter to Lady Croom	91	Burned by Septimus (p. 96)
Septimus's letter to Thomasina	91	Burned by Septimus (p. 96)
Byron's letter to Septimus	93	Burned by Septimus, unread (p. 94)
Thomasina's drawing book	103	(Fate unknown)
Prize Scientific Academy essay of 1812	105	(Fate unknown) (p. 108)
Thomasina's diagram of heat exchange	113	Septimus's portfolio (p. 56)
Picture of Septimus with Plautus drawn by Thomasina	116	Given to Septimus, then to Augustus; found by Gus and given to Hannah
Thomasina's final alpha essay	122	(Fate unknown; burned?)

The list tells us about the kinds of evidence that are preserved and the circumstances in which they are. 'Why were things saved, do you think?' Hannah pertinently asks (p. 58). Things are saved, and evidence is preserved, owing to a mixture of factors. The old families who own country houses typically have a strong sense of continuity and history. They also have the space to keep things undisturbed that have no apparent value — hence the survival of so many items in the house, either in the library or elsewhere. Valentine comments that the game books are 'My true inheritance. Two hundred years of real data on a plate' (p. 61). Other surviving documents are in the form of letters. This suggests that they are the most likely written texts to be preserved by their recipients, but this begs various questions about why some are destroyed, like Septimus's letters to Lady Croom and Thomasina, and whether this is evidence of chance or design. A further problem with notes or letters beginning 'Sir' is that unless the envelope is also preserved, which they are not in the case of the first set of three letters, the identity of the recipient can be in doubt. Misfortune is also a great destroyer; the fire that consumed Thomasina no doubt also accounted for many of her papers, including her final alpha essay. Note also that on p. 76 Bernard invents 'a platonic letter which confirms everything' — which is doubly ironic, because there *was* such a letter, burned by Septimus without reading it (p. 94), but it confirms a very different story from the one that Bernard is assuming. Pictures tend to survive, but have the potential to be misattributed to their artists or subjects, and even essays were often published anonymously or pseudonymously. The survival of evidence is therefore unpredictable and can be misleading.

Chaos Theory

An apparently trivial event may have important, far-reaching and unpredictable consequences. An excellent example is Lady Croom borrowing Septimus's copy of *The Couch of Eros* to lend to Byron. A predictable consequence is that Septimus never sees his book again; a totally unpredictable and 'chaotic' consequence is that Bernard believes he has found proof that Byron wrote the dismissive reviews of Chater's poems in the *Piccadilly Recreation*, which he makes a key part of his argument for his erroneous assumption that Byron shot Chater in a duel. This conclusion is triply wrong: Byron did not write the reviews, Chater did *not* die at Sidley Park and there *was* no duel. If there had been, it would have been with Septimus although, as a further irony, Byron actually *did* have sex with Mrs Chater, and Mr Chater might well have called him out (as he did with Septimus) had Byron not fled in the early hours.

Another example is the apparent *acte gratuit* of Thomasina drawing a hermit in the hermitage in Noakes's sketch book (p. 18), making him 'like the Baptist in the wilderness' (p. 19), which causes ripples of effect down the centuries. (We presume that the idea of becoming the hermit was planted in Septimus's mind at this point and came to fruition as a result of his grief over Thomasina's death.)

The Couch of Eros

```
┌─────────────────────────────────────────────────┐
│           Septimus has it to review it          │
└─────────────────────────────────────────────────┘
                        ↓
┌─────────────────────────────────────────────────┐
│   Septimus underlines points while writing review│
└─────────────────────────────────────────────────┘
                        ↓
┌─────────────────────────────────────────────────┐
│         Septimus places three letters in it     │
└─────────────────────────────────────────────────┘
                        ↓
┌─────────────────────────────────────────────────┐
│              Lady Croom borrows it              │
└─────────────────────────────────────────────────┘
                        ↓
┌─────────────────────────────────────────────────┐
│           Lady Croom lends it to Byron          │
└─────────────────────────────────────────────────┘
                        ↓
┌─────────────────────────────────────────────────┐
│     Byron leaves Sidley Park suddenly, taking it│
└─────────────────────────────────────────────────┘
                        ↓
┌─────────────────────────────────────────────────┐
│        Contents of Byron's house sold in 1816   │
└─────────────────────────────────────────────────┘
                        ↓
┌─────────────────────────────────────────────────┐
│   Book bought by the bookseller John Nightingale,│
│                Bernard's ancestor                │
└─────────────────────────────────────────────────┘
                        ↓
┌─────────────────────────────────────────────────┐
│      Book moved to Nightingale house in Kent    │
│                    in 1939                       │
└─────────────────────────────────────────────────┘
                        ↓
┌─────────────────────────────────────────────────┐
│   Building of Channel Tunnel forces demolition   │
│                   of house                       │
└─────────────────────────────────────────────────┘
                        ↓
┌─────────────────────────────────────────────────┐
│       Book found and acquired by Bernard,       │
│                 owner's cousin                   │
└─────────────────────────────────────────────────┘
                        ↓
┌─────────────────────────────────────────────────┐
│   Bernard assumes three enclosed letters were    │
│                written to Byron                  │
└─────────────────────────────────────────────────┘
                        ↓
┌─────────────────────────────────────────────────┐
│   Bernard interprets underlinings as evidence Byron│
│                  wrote review                    │
└─────────────────────────────────────────────────┘
                        ↓
┌─────────────────────────────────────────────────┐
│   Bernard visits Sidley Park in 1993, looking for│
│                evidence of duel                  │
└─────────────────────────────────────────────────┘
                        ↓
┌─────────────────────────────────────────────────┐
│   Bernard gives talk based on these mistaken     │
│   assumptions, claiming Byron killed Chater      │
└─────────────────────────────────────────────────┘
```

Structural doubles

In addition to the pairing of characters and the number of props that feature in pairs, and the pairings of thematic opposites (e.g. paradise and death), there are also structural doubles built into the framework of the play, beginning, obviously, with the parallel time periods.

Ownership of objects

Ownership of objects transfers from one character to another:

- Byron's pistols become the property of Septimus.
- Augustus's hare is claimed by Byron.
- Chater's duel with Septimus becomes Brice's as well.
- Mrs Chater becomes Mrs Brice.
- Septimus's book reviews are attributed to Byron.
- Thomasina appropriates Septimus's maths primer and writes in it.
- Septimus's copy of *The Couch of Eros* becomes Byron's.
- Thomasina's sketch passes from Septimus to Augustus (in 1812).
- Thomasina's sketch passes from Gus to Hannah (present day).

Repeated events

Events happen twice, another form of duplication:

- Chater challenges Septimus twice.
- Septimus writes two book reviews of Chater's poems.
- There are two banishments by jealous Lady Crooms (Byron and Bernard).
- Two teenagers want to learn the facts of life from Septimus (Thomasina and Augustus).
- Two teenagers have a crush on a teacher figure (Thomasina and Chloë).
- Two teenagers are learning to play the piano (Thomasina and Gus).
- Two reviewers write scathing reviews (Septimus and Bernard).
- Lady Croom asks Thomasina how old she is twice.
- A tortoise is fed twice.
- Hannah is writing a book on Sidley Park's garden, having previously described Caroline Lamb's, so her double endeavour directly connects the two periods.

Bisociation

Two fields being put into chance association — what Koestler calls '**bisociation**' — is a key philosophical concept in the play, the main example being desserts and maths; it leads to discovery, the '**Eureka**' outcome. Putting together 1809 and the present day — the intuition plus the technology to prove it — provides a satisfying synthesis. A theorem or theory can be proved or disproved, and the many claims and disputes over these in the play hold the plot and dialogues in tension, as do the concepts of before and after, and heat versus cold, which are dichotomies in everything from a night of passion that goes wrong to the way the world will end.

Structural triples

There are almost no characters in the play, in either period, who are not involved sexually or romantically with at least two others, thus forming constantly shifting patterns (fractals) and triangles (geometry). The non-duel (involving three people: the cause and the combatants) is at the heart of the plot, as are the two sets of three letters (one set survives, the other set is burned). There are actually three time periods, the first of which covers three days and the second of which is a three-year jump from the first. The three stages of the landscaping of Sidley Park are discussed and compared. There are three maths issues: Fermat, thermodynamics and iterative functions. In the first six scenes the periods 1809 and present day alternate three times. The waltz is famously in triple time, and mirrors the triplings of the plot: there are three kisses between Septimus and Thomasina (pp. 107, 122 and 127), and three occasions of sexual impropriety commented on, in the gazebo/hermitage/cottage.

In science, art and nature the number three is significant: it is a primary and magic number; thirds are the classical ratio for aesthetic proportion; there are three primary colours; three is the minimum number of lines to make a geometric shape, a complete containing figure and one with ancient associations with preservation, aspiration and mystical properties. The Bible and literature, folklore and mythology, all make use of this key number, which betokens both unity and division, and therefore **comedy** and **tragedy**.

The changing garden

Gardens are a traditional feature of western literature going back to their roots in the Bible, mythology and medieval **fabliaux** and romances. Many works of fiction, Victorian and more modern, are set in or make use of a garden, as do Shakespeare's comedies in the form of a 'green world'. Changes in literary taste coincided with changes in country estate landscapes during the eighteenth-century progression from the **Enlightenment** to the Romantic period.

The three phases of Sidley Park

The landscaping of the garden of Sidley Park is central to the play. Sidley Park comprises 500 acres and had been a formal Italianate garden until 1740. By identifying references in the text, made by Hannah and Lady Croom in particular, we can record the changing features and aspect of the garden since then.

'The Gothic novel expressed in landscape'

The picturesque stage of the garden reflects the contemporary **Gothic** novel, also referred to in the play. Gothic novels and Romantic poetry (see Coleridge's 'Kubla

Phase 1: Sidley Park, Derbyshire 1809

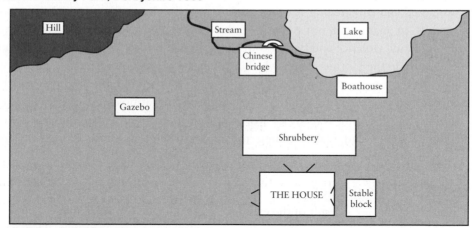

Phase 2: Sidley Park, Derbyshire 1812

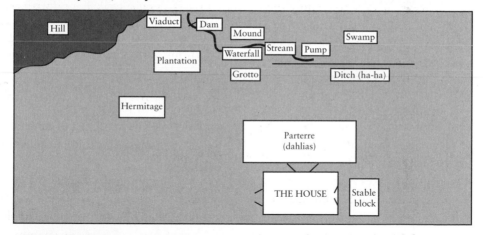

Phase 3: Sidley Park, Derbyshire 1993

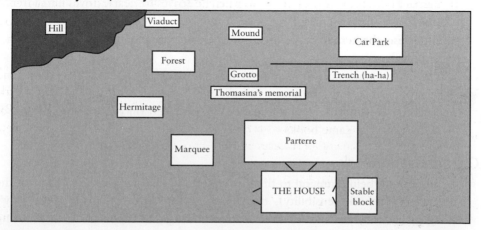

Khan') depicted wild and uncontrollable passions, which in landscape terms meant untamed and threatening features, nature as a dominant force, which is 'measureless to man' and not subject to his control or even his understanding. Irregularity, violence and darkness were the characteristics of both landscape and literature in the Gothic **genre**, which also shared the same spectacular settings of woods and caves, chasms and ruins. Shadows and moonlight, rather than the reassuring presence of daylight, were the presiding atmospheres; the perpetual gloom and looming tragedy of works of fiction and garden design minimised human power and scale, leading to an overwhelming sense of decline and impending doom.

Products of the garden

Various events are a result of the existence and influence of the garden:

- Mrs Chater finds the gazebo a convenient place to seduce Septimus. They have also had sex in the boathouse.
- Noakes uses his theodolite to be, in effect, a voyeur in the garden.
- Byron goes out shooting and falsely claims to have killed a hare, thus pretending to have a skill he does not possess and showing a disregard for facts, which deceives history as represented by Bernard.
- Septimus spends a night in the boathouse waiting for a duel.
- Septimus shoots a rabbit for Thomasina and gives it to Jellaby.
- Thomasina uses an apple leaf from the garden as her inspiration and model for iterative equations. Septimus and Plautus eat the apple. Her rabbit equation which 'eats its own progeny' is also a garden image.
- Septimus takes Augustus into the garden to tell him about the facts of life.
- Thomasina and Septimus kiss in the hermitage.
- Hannah goes out to compare the garden with the sketch book, which is why she is not there when Bernard arrives.
- Bernard is irritated by the garden, as when he arrives he nearly drives into a trench (the former ha-ha).
- Chloë uses the hermitage for a secret sexual assignation with Bernard; her mother snoops there.
- The annual fancy-dress party is held in a marquee. People usually get drunk and behave badly at this event.
- Valentine is using the data the garden has provided on grouse populations, as recorded in the game books.

Garden framework

In addition to being integral to the play's **plot** and **characterisation** (a test of the characters' aesthetic sensibility), the garden is the source of much of the play's **imagery** and is a **symbol** of its main **themes**: change, as explored by the debating of the relative merits of neo-classicical and Romantic views of life; sexual attraction, which is in turn representative of Chaos Theory; the link between nature and science (as represented by the steam pump, for instance). Ultimately, and paradoxically, gardens are, however well it is disguised, the product of a combination of science and art, an artificial creation not a natural one. Generally, gardens are associated with growth, beauty and therefore life, but death, danger and fornication occur in the grounds of Sidley Park.

The fact that the gazebo became the hermitage and is now called the cottage shows that words may change but basic human behaviours do not. By its very existence the garden encourages illicit sexual activity in the play, for practical reasons in that it provides secrecy — or characters mistakenly think it does — and because of its symbolism as the producer of apples and therefore the temptation. As in Genesis, sins committed in the garden are found out, immediately, and judged. Eviction from Eden, the fate of Adam and Eve after their first coupling, is the fate of the Chaters and their companions when they are expelled from Sidley Park.

From medieval literature onwards, the garden, representing the beauty and fertility of nature, has been an artistic and literary allegory of the female body, hence the need to wall and gate it, and for there to be only one key for chastity to be ensured; ways were then inevitably found to get around the restriction of access. (As late as Jane Austen's *Mansfield Park*, the idea of the locked garden gate to mean chastity was still being used.)

The garden produces the game, the birds and the hares that are shot down by the house guests for amusement. This provides a symbol of casual death, the introduction of evil into paradise. The changing nature of the garden represents constant flux, time moving on, creating and destroying as it goes along, as new fashions and philosophies replace the old, and the old become new again. But the line of the arrow from sex to death is constant: in literature (e.g. **Antony and Cleopatra**), in theology (Genesis to Apocalypse), in history (Caroline Lamb) — and in this play (Thomasina kisses Septimus, in the garden, then dies).

Sex, literature and death at Sidley Park

Sex, literature and death, linked by a headline, can be associated with large gardens, places where nature reproduces and covert couplings take place, where poets are inspired to create verse, where poison is administered or creatures attack the unarmed and unsuspecting. The Fall of Man in the Garden of Eden, the story of the end of innocence and the beginning of experience, knowledge and mortality, has inspired western literature for centuries. The play also owes something to the

traditional **genres** of the country-house **drama** and the country-house detective story: in the first there is an exploration of family, class and relationships between guests and hosts, much misunderstanding and much coming and going of characters; in the second there is a sudden suspicious death or disappearance and many mysteries and clues to be solved.

The garden is more than just a setting; it is a suitable backdrop for creation and destruction, relationships forged and broken, as in the original Garden of Eden. It is a paradise — 'nature as God intended' — that is threatened by modernity and human invasion. Its visitors in both periods are associated with literature, and they also avail themselves of the sexual opportunities on offer; people shut up in remote houses often get bored, feel deprived and become over-expansive when people arrive from the outside world. The play makes a point of connecting gardening and writing wherever possible, as for example in the confused reference to Horace Walpole (known for both his gardening essay and his **Gothic** novel) and the role of Caroline Lamb as lover, novelist and garden owner. Hannah directly links gardens with books, being herself a biographer and garden historian. In that shooting takes place throughout the play, that a duel is planned in the earlier period and referred to throughout, and that Thomasina burns to death in her bedroom, the Park's link to death is clear, though ironically not in the way that Bernard believed when the headline 'Even in Arcadia — Sex, Literature and Death at Sidley Park' was written. Sexual attraction and sudden death are random factors that interfere with predictability and spoil theories.

Death in the play

The following **allusions** are made to death:

- The game books are referred to as 'a calendar of slaughter'.
- Gunfire is heard in both periods.
- Chater proposes a rendezvous in the gunroom.
- A double duel is arranged.
- Byron's pistols are confiscated because he is dangerous with them.
- There is a dispute about who shot a hare.
- The appearance of an apple is a reminder of **the Fall**, punished by death.
- Noakes is the serpent in the garden, i.e. Satan, the bringer of death to Eden.
- A dead rabbit with blood on it is brought into the house.
- 'Phoeey to death', says Thomasina hubristically.
- Thomasina perishes in a fire.
- Chater dies of a monkey bite in the West Indies in 1810.
- 'Rabbits eating their own progeny' is Thomasina's example of an iterated algorithm.
- Septimus suffered a decline and died in the hermitage in 1834.

- The present-day Coverlys are a reminder of their dead ancestors.
- The garden has been destroyed to satisfy whim, folly and pretension.
- 'We are all doomed', as the universe is dying.

Play characters and sex, literature and death

An interest in sex is shared by nearly all the characters and is particularly represented by Septimus, Mrs Chater, Lady Croom and Bernard, who are all connected to literature in some way, as readers, writers or would-be lovers of would-be writers. In addition, Captain Brice pays for the publication of Chater's poetry and indirectly brings about his demise, on account of his sexual passion for his wife.

Thomasina is undergoing a sexual awakening, will become one of the subjects of Hannah's next book *The Genius of the Place* and will die tragically at Sidley Park. She seeks carnal knowledge and talks of sin, the wages of which are death.

Lady Croom's mistranslation of '*Et in Arcadia ego*' as 'Here I am in Arcadia', taking on the persona of death, draws attention to her role as judge in Sidley Park, and the play even seems to suggest that she sentences Thomasina to death. Like God's voice in the Garden of Eden, she expels those who have gained too much knowledge. (Brice says 'If that was not God speaking through Lady Croom, he never spoke through anyone!' p. 55.) She has the power of banishment after a 'night of reckoning', i.e. a day of judgement.

Chater is also a strong link to the three main topics, with his erotic poetic works, nymphomaniac wife, predilection for duels and his fatal encounter with a monkey. His belief that it is appropriate to shoot someone for sexual impropriety is on a par with Bernard's that it was appropriate to shoot someone for writing a bad review of one's literary work.

Hannah accuses Bernard of being obsessed with these topics: 'Sex and literature. Literature and sex. Your conversation…doesn't have many places to go' (p. 84).

Historical characters and sex, literature and death

As a poet infamous for his sexual exploits and famous for his untimely death while fighting for the revolutionary cause in Greece, Byron is the most obvious connection between sex and literature and death, which were actually fairly widespread obsessions of the Romantic period he represents (making it ironic that the anti-Romantic Bernard should share them). The older Thomasina finds him physically attractive and claims to want to marry him, but Byron is mentioned as often in connection with dead hares and pistols as he is with women and poetry, and his poem 'Darkness' (p. 105) links him to the death of the universe as well as the death of Thomasina, since they have shared the vision of the world being doomed.

Lady Caroline Lamb was a spurned mistress and writer who died tragically and prematurely.

D. H. Lawrence is referred to in scene 2, another seducer of married women in real life and the notorious author of scandalous, sexually explicit novels, the most prominent being *Lady Chatterley's Lover* and *Women in Love*, in which accidental death as well as sex feature prominently.

Queen Cleopatra of Egypt is discussed in scene 3; this historical figure is one of Shakespeare's tragic heroines, the cause of her own death and Antony's, as well as being a legendary figure representing the epitome of female sexual allure.

Sir Isaac Newton is an unexpected link between sex and death in that he discovered gravity by observing the fall of an apple.

Madness and sex, literature and death

The play contains and refers to poets, lunatics and lovers; in *A Midsummer Night's Dream* Shakespeare grouped these as sharing the kind of madness that is the result of an excess of imagination. Caroline Lamb (writer and mistress) is believed to have gone mad or had a nervous breakdown, which led to her death; Byron (poet and serial seducer) was described as 'mad' by Caroline Lamb and was the son of 'Mad Jack'. This pair of lovers, conjoined in the portrait cover of Hannah's book, are the historical spirits who preside over Sidley Park and its garden. Septimus (reviewer, ladies' man and Byron's friend) dies as a lunatic hermit the same year as the other 'bad' Romantic poet, Coleridge (opium addict given to hallucinations), whose most famous work is that of a mariner sent mad by his supernatural voyage. A belief that the end of the world is nigh and can be predicted (the Sidley Park hermit was engaged in 'proofs the world was coming to an end') is a traditional way that madness takes characters in literature — and not only in literature. Pan, the rapacious **satyr** who gave his name to the madness called panic, seems to be a presence in Sidley Park, as in Arcadia.

In the modern generation, Bernard, who has sex on the brain, and who is involved in literature as a teacher, essayist and researcher of Byron, commits professional suicide by publishing a mad theory, despite many warnings not to. Gus is mad in the sense of abnormal and eccentric, linked to sex to the extent of committing the act of Eve in offering Hannah an apple, and although not directly literary himself, as far as we know, is the repository of information about the literary characters of Sidley Park. He is the resurrected Augustus and seems to hover between the periods and the characters like an omniscient ghost, neither dead nor fully alive, trapped in the past and not speaking in the present.

The genius of the place

The Latin phrase *genius loci* (meaning 'spirit of the place' and used by Pope in his 'Epistle to Lord Burlington') links classical mythology with the **pantheistic** beliefs of the Romantic era, and the Romantic era with the contemporary academic research into the history of the house and garden, thus connecting the three eras represented in the play. It is a short Romantic step from believing in gods and **nymphs** inhabiting wild areas of landscape to wanting to have one in one's newly untamed garden, and so it was that hermits or *genii* (analogous to the *genie* of Arabian and *djinn* of Indian tales) were advertised for and employed in late eighteenth- and early nineteenth-century England (not always successfully). Hermits — otherwise known as recluses, eremites and prophets — were required to be picturesque, showing man's essential wildness and his subjugation to his environment. They have a bibilical heritage (see Thomasina on John the Baptist) as well as a Romantic literary one (e.g. Coleridge's hermit in 'The Ancient Mariner' and Heathcliff in *Wuthering Heights*).

The other, more modern, meaning of genius as prodigy is also relevant to *Arcadia*; and Hannah's next book is to be called *The Genius of the Place*, exploiting the **pun**. Both meanings convey a sense of the supernatural. There is more than one claimant to the title of genius of Sidley Park, as well as a mystery about the identity of its hermit, who is both a spirit of the place and a savant working on a highly intellectual task. As the poet Dryden put it: 'great wit to madness sure is near allied', i.e. there is a only a thin line between genius and lunacy, so hermits and reclusive academics were often thought to be mad, and this is also what connects the two meanings of genius: solitary existence tends to produce the effect of madness, e.g. talking to oneself, even if eccentricity is not already evident in those seeking such an abnormal life. Hannah personifies the Romantic movement as 'A mind in chaos suspected of genius', thus linking two key words in the play and drawing attention to the apparently similar manifestations of chaos and genius.

Characters of genius

Fermat was a genius: all his theorems have proved to be true. Newton is viewed as a genius because of his brilliant insights, which shaped science for centuries. Bernard calls Byron a genius twice (p. 72 and p. 79). Byron's 'Darkness' poem seems to prefigure entropy, thereby opening a door in a house not yet built.

Bernard would like to think that he himself is 'touched by genius', but no one else would agree. Hannah is able to prove her theory about the hermit, and her instinct about the (fictional) Fuseli sketch being of Byron and Caroline Lamb proves correct. However, these require common intelligence rather than an exceptional gift; she is not especially talented, just thorough. Valentine is very able and can understand Thomasina's heat exchange diagram, but does not have the tenacity or patience to count as a genius, judging by his giving up on his grouse studies, his mind not being readily open to 'thinking outside the box' and the fact that at nearly 30 he is already too old to qualify.

The three fictional characters who could claim genius, and have it claimed for them, are Septimus, Thomasina and Gus. Hannah calls Septimus 'the genius of Sidley Park' (p. 88) and Valentine thinks Thomasina 'had a genius for her tutor' (p. 104). His becoming a hermit and going mad would fit the **stereotype**; 'he was suspected of genius' and of being 'off his head'. However, Septimus makes no intellectual breakthroughs of his own, whereas Thomasina, though very young and not yet fully educated, is already capable of original thought and discovery, and is therefore a prodigy, which is Hannah's view of her.

One must not forget Gus, though he is easily overlooked by characters on stage and by the audience. He is dumb, and the absence of a faculty has often been associated with outstanding creative gifts, as indeed has childhood trauma. He is the silent presence at Sidley Park and the presiding spirit of the house and garden, who intuitively knows and understands everything about the place and the people in it, past and present. He has studied all the 'old stuff' and understood its significance. Chloë describes Gus as 'my genius brother' (p. 45) and gives the example of his mysterious knowledge of the whereabouts of the foundations of the former boathouse. He can improvise music on the piano, and brings the knowledge of Thomasina and Septimus to Hannah through an apple leaf and a lost picture.

The play's view of genius

The characters of genius show an ability to cross the mental and temperamental divides between art and science, passion and rationality, in a way that the audience are asked to approve of and admire. The desire to find things out, the patience and objectivity to collect the evidence, and the determination to commit to the chase are admirable characteristics that give validity to human existence; as Hannah puts it, 'It's wanting to know that makes us matter' (p. 100). The ability to live out of one's own time (which Thomasina and Gus have) is the gift of unlimited perspective. Genius is being the first person to ask the question, of knowing how to do things without ever having been taught, of opening a door before there is a house. However, it carries penalities and liabilities, and seems to be a gift that has to be paid for: being misunderstood and mocked and unrecognised in one's own lifetime, and, in literature at least, being punished by death for having acquired excessive knowledge or having been too different. Thomasina's fate would bear this out. Despite being so clever and so dedicated, Septimus actually wasted his life and achieved nothing. Taking a gloomy view, the real spirit of the place is Death, who haunts the play from before the beginning to after the end, and in historical terms from Arcadia through Eden to the predicted end of the world.

Mystery, discovery and knowledge

The play is in interrogative mode, beginning with Thomasina's opening question about the facts of life, and it embraces many different kinds of enquiry. Historical mysteries are alluded to in the play, such as the riddle of the sphinx and the burning of the great library of Alexandria; Fermat's Last Theorem was also used by Stoppard in that capacity, but ironically that mystery was solved two months after the first performance of the play in April 1993. Frustration with an insoluble mystery has long been accepted as a cause of madness (see Thomasina's claim that Fermat only pretended to have a solution to make all future mathematicians mad) and thus mystery, madness, hermits, genius, discovery and knowledge are all linked.

Many mysteries

The play is, on one level, a mystery/crime story, the detective fiction **genre** that Stoppard used in his earlier plays, *After Magritte*, *The Real Inspector Hound* and *Jumpers*. Was a murder committed at Sidley Park, and if not, where was Byron during those missing three days, and why did he flee the country?

Literary critics are detectives in various ways: they solve the clues of textual interpretation; they identify authors and material; they engage in biographical reconstruction.

The play is also a scientific enquiry and it questions fundamental principles of human behaviour and destiny, seeking to solve the mystery of the universe, no less. Valentine is engrossed in trying to detect a pattern in the fluctuations of animal populations.

An earlier mathematical mystery given to Thomasina to solve was that of finding a proof for Fermat's Last Theorem, which was called 'the most tantalising problem in the history of mathematics'. She instead embarks upon solving other mathematical mysteries, in particular that of how to get nature to give up its numerical secrets.

History is a mystery, as the play makes clear on many occasions; reconstructing the past is like solving a puzzle. Thomasina's **dictum** is: 'We must work outward from the middle of the maze' (p. 49). Bernard's is, less helpfully: 'You'd have to be there' (p. 64).

The facts of life are a mystery into which children have to be initiated at some stage. Sexual attraction is a mystery. Is it chemical, so that it can be described one day by a formula as yet undiscovered, or will it remain for ever beyond rational explanation, and therefore unpredictable?

Thomasina asks whether carnal embrace is a sin, thereby touching on the theological debate concerning **the Fall** and the paradoxes of the existence of evil in a pre-lapsarian world and the impossibility of falling unless one is already fallen. The

universe continues to supply humans with mysteries: 'what happens in a cup of coffee when the cream goes in — these things are full of mystery, as mysterious to us as the heavens were to the Greeks' (p. 62–63).

Many questions

The play's characters have questions, and reasons for asking them:

- **Bernard:** why did Lord Byron leave England so suddenly in 1809? He wants to be famous.
- **Hannah:** who was the hermit of Sidley Park? She wants to do a thorough job of researching the garden.
- **Valentine:** what is the formula for variations in grouse population? He wants a PhD.
- **Thomasina:** is there an equation for nature's numbers? She wants to be the first person to ask, and to find the answer.
- **Septimus:** is the universe doomed to grow cold? He has an intellectual need to know.

What the audience want to know

The audience's interests are different. Because of their historical perspective, they know about Fermat's Last Theorem (just!) and about the Second Law of Thermodynamics. They are not particularly anxious to know why Byron left England in 1809, as this is of limited specialist interest. They are interested, however, in knowing the identity of the Sidley Park hermit because they are on the side of Hannah, because they guess it might involve the two most attractive characters, Septimus and Thomasina, and because they feel part of the mystery in that they witnessed the 'creation' of the hermit. The audience are engaged enough with the play's characters to wonder how serious the feelings between Septimus and Thomasina are, whether Bernard will come unstuck with his theory, and why Gus can't speak and whether he will by the end of the play. Stoppard quite deliberately teases the reader about this in his stage directions: '*Gus doesn't speak. He never speaks. Perhaps he cannot speak*' (p. 22). When we learn in scene 7 that Thomasina dies in a fire on the eve of her seventeenth birthday, we want to know how it came about.

The identity of the hermit

Below are the stages by which clues to the identity of the hermit of Sidley Park are presented to the audience:

- Thomasina draws a hermit on Noakes's sketch book (scene 1).
- Hannah explains to Bernard that the hermit was mad and spent his time trying to prove that 'the world was coming to an end' (scene 2).
- Thomasina and Septimus discuss her algebra (scene 3).

- Hannah and Valentine discuss the possibility that Thomasina discovered iterated algorithms (scene 4).
- Peacock's letter describes a lunatic hermit at Sidley Park who had only a pet tortoise for a companion and who believed the world was losing its light and life. The male pronoun is used, and in any case there is no precedent for a female hermit (scene 5).
- Septimus uses the flame of the spirit lamp to destroy his own letters. The hermit's papers were set fire to (scene 6).
- Septimus reacts with concern to being told by Thomasina that the 'Improved Newtonian Universe must cease and grow cold' (scene 7).
- Lady Croom and Noakes discuss the need for a hermit. At the same time Thomasina sketches Septimus with Plautus (scene 7).
- Septimus says to Thomasina: 'It will make me mad as you promised' (scene 7).
- Augustus asks Septimus for permission to keep Thomasina's sketch (scene 7).
- Gus gives Hannah the folio containing the picture of Septimus and tortoise, to reveal to Hannah the only possible identity of the hermit (scene 7).

Does Thomasina already know the facts of life?

This question has caused much debate among critics. Her brother, who is 15, still does not know the facts of life so there is no reason to suppose that Thomasina is being disingenuous in her opening question to Septimus, and her mother's horror that she may have found out would support her being ignorant and innocent at the start of the play. Her bewilderment is signified by her '*puzzled frown*' in the stage directions and counters the argument that Thomasina is teasing and embarrassing Septimus, as does her response when she does finally learn the true answer: 'Eurghhh!'

She admits to having suspected that carnal embrace means 'kissing', and we presume that if she had known more she would have said so, being a character who enjoys showing off what she knows. Someone who finds the idea of sex 'disgusting and incomprehensible' is unlikely to be pretending to be coy, and this is further belied by the stage direction that has Thomasina running off into the garden as '*an uncomplicated girl*'. Septimus also confirms that 'She speaks from innocence not from experience'. It is therefore difficult to find a case for her already knowing the facts of life when the play commences. What is certain is that she is ready to be told, and that this has been triggered by the servants' report of what happened in the gazebo between Septimus and Mrs Chater, and is symbolised by the incursion into the garden by the unwitting serpent, Noakes.

Chater and Byron

The real version of what happened between Chater and Byron is that although Byron was indeed at Sidley Park at the same time as Chater, the duel was to be between Chater and Septimus, and both Chater and Byron were forced to leave, separately, by Lady Croom before any duel could take place. Septimus's copy of *The Couch of Eros* found its way into Byron's library because Lady Croom borrowed it from Septimus to lend it to Byron, who then left suddenly without returning it. The letter he left behind for Septimus, which the latter did not read, may have alluded to this. Hannah explodes the myth of Byron the murderer by discovering the true date and mode of Chater's death in a letter from Lady Croom to her husband, which refers to Chater's discovery of a new breed of dahlia in Martinique and Brice's marriage to the widow Chater.

Bernard's theory, however, is rather different. Bernard found Septimus's copy of *The Couch of Eros*, containing Chater's letters of challenge to Septimus, in the book stock of a relative, and traced it back to Byron's library at Newstead. However, the letters were not addressed to anyone by name, and Bernard erroneously assumes that Chater summoned Byron to a duel because the latter had criticised his poems as well as seduced his wife. He further assumes that the duel took place, that Byron killed Chater, and that Byron then had to flee the country to escape the consequences. He wants to believe 'Bonking Byron Shot Poet' in order to pull off a scholarly scoop.

Who shot the hare?

This is a minor mystery, but a paradigm for all **whodunnits**, and one symptomatic of the problem of falsification of evidence; it is also a question that has caused a rift between distinguished German critics of the play. Both Byron and Augustus claim the hare; we are inclined to believe the latter because Bernard is wrong about his main premise that Byron shot Chater, so it would be logical for him to be wrong about this too. Doubt about Byron is created by other characters too; Lady Croom, who is factually wrong on several occasions in the play, attributes a pigeon to Byron in the first scene which is then reassigned to Augustus, prefiguring the later false claim. Septimus corrects her and says 'my schoolfriend was never a sportsman', and he should know. Brice then confirms that Augustus shot it, and not Byron. Later Lady Croom asks Septimus to take Byron's pistols away from him as he is not safe with them. Septimus says that Byron is a 'poor shot' and it seems that Byron's claim to the hare rests only on the **pun** of 'a hare's breadth'.

However, Septimus puts Byron down on several other occasions and their relationship is competitive; they are rivals as both lovers and writers of reviews. Septimus tells Thomasina he 'was better at this than Lord Byron' when translating Latin, at the same time as proving himself capable of being as much of a cheat (he is using Shakespeare's version for his translation of Plutarch), so we cannot be totally sure about the reliability of his judgement of his schoolfriend, and in fact he never has a good word to say about Byron. There are other occasions when Septimus evinces jealousy of those in receipt of Lady Croom's sexual favour; he puts Count Zelinsky down at every opportunity and Lady Croom thinks that Septimus is sulking because of Zelinsky, so perhaps the audience are meant to believe that he is equally capable of sulking because of Byron, and that therefore his opinions of him are suspect. Furthermore, Septimus has reason to bear a grudge against Byron, since the latter thoughtlessly revealed to Chater at breakfast the authorship of the review, thus bringing about the second of Chater's challenges.

On balance, the fact that Bernard says '[Byron] wrote those lines as sure as he shot that hare', when he did not write the lines, seems to be a clear indicator to the audience that Byron did not shoot the hare either; since the two hypotheses have been linked, the falsity of one necessitates that the other half of the equation is equally false, according to mathematical principles.

Remaining mysteries

Some answers have still not been provided by the end of the play. Ironically, the original mystery of why Byron left England still remains. We do not know what was in Byron's letter to Septimus, which the latter burned without reading, but must assume that it referred to more than just his intention to take *The Couch of Eros* with him, as that hardly seems of sufficient import for someone to write a letter about in the middle of the night. Of course, had the letter survived and been found, Bernard could never have started off on his false trail, so when he asserts later that 'letters get lost' there is dramatic irony for the audience to enjoy.

Likewise, we never learn what happened to Gus when he was five that made him stop speaking, or why he 'hates people shouting' (p. 68).

The audience are also left with the question of whether Thomasina's prophecy came true; Septimus tells her in scene 7: 'It will make me mad as you promised.' Hermits and scientists were stereotypically regarded as eccentric to the point of lunacy (see Dr Frankenstein), but the Septimus we see shows no signs of incipient insanity. We also do not know whether he was trying to prove or disprove the law of entropy. Peacock is quoted (fictionally) as saying that the hermit was labouring for 'the restitution of hope through good English algebra' (p. 87) but scene 2 refers to his 'proofs the world was coming to an end'. And if he did really go mad, as opposed to just wanting time and space to pursue his calculations, was it from despair about the fate of the universe or grief about Thomasina's death, and if the latter, was the grief also mixed with guilt? What were his feelings for Thomasina, before and after her death? What happened in Thomasina's room that night? Why did she leave her candle alight, despite warning, and set fire to her room? Is it significant that he lit the candle for her? Was she expecting Septimus to come to her despite his saying that he would not, and fell asleep with the candle still lit while waiting? Why did he kiss her if he was not going to do more than that? Did he come to her room and seduce her, and was the candle knocked over by accident? Did he leave her to her fate in order to save himself, or to avoid being found in her room?

And if her death was a punishment, was it for her precocious mathematical talent or her promiscuity?

Rediscovery

Septimus claims that lost knowledge can always be rediscovered. He is not the only one who believes in shedding and picking up, as Bernard exclaims: 'It dropped from sight but we will write it again!' (p. 65). It would thus appear to be Stoppard's own optimistic view, which sounds convincing in Septimus's passionate set speech on page 50.

The Couch of Eros resurfaces 180 years after it is borrowed, and Septimus's maths primer and Thomasina's maths book, as well as her drawing of Septimus, are 'found' in Sidley Park. Gus plays an important role as the custodian of artefacts and historical facts. Thomasina's maths is rediscovered by Mandelbrot (historically) and Valentine (fictionally). The solution to Fermat's Last Theorem was announced during the play's first run. It appears that in certain circumstances knowledge, unlike paradise, can be regained.

'Discovery by misadventure'

This is Koestler's term for when new knowledge is stumbled upon through the process of '**bisociation**', the associative and non-logical linking of apparently unrelated systems, like jam in rice pudding and entropy (for Archimedes it was mass and bathwater). Discoveries can also be made by chance, sheer serendipity, as when Bernard finds Septimus's portfolio in a library cupboard when he is actually looking for something else.

Discoverers

The play suggests that discovery belongs to people who are witty, intelligent and educated, able to take on board new ideas and modify previous positions, who are daring enough to break rules and experiment (to 'think aside' as the German critic Niederhoff puts it), and who are genuinely interested in truth for its own sake. Science needs a basis of agreed knowledge to be able to progress, but equally, knowledge is never absolute and may need to be rejected when new data, perspectives and approaches become available, when everything we thought we knew turns out to be untrue. That Septimus follows Thomasina's thinking, and Valentine follows Hannah's, unusually makes the females the pioneers in this play.

Scientific discovery requires sufficient time, and space, and a reason for doing it, and someone with the passion and commitment to keep working at the problem. And technology helps: Stoppard shows how computers can do the repetitive work in a fraction of the time, and how they have made new forms of study possible, such as stylistic analysis. However, the inspiration for what to investigate and what to compare must still originate from human intuition. Septimus, Bernard, Thomasina,

Valentine and Hannah — all the main characters from both periods — each have a theory, some more than one (Bernard also has a theory about ha-has). Sometimes the unlikely answer is actually the correct one (see p. 75), so nothing should ever be ruled out in advance. However, as Septimus tartly points out, 'A fancy is not a discovery' (p. 49) and as Bernard advises, ironically since he does not do it, 'you have to turn over every page' before you announce that you have discovered the truth.

As presented in the play, historical research is both a science and an art: inspiration is needed to construct a theory; rigorous pursuit and analysis of evidence must follow; writing the subsequent book requires literary skill. Bernard is clearly insufficiently scientific, as he leaps to unsupported conclusions. Hannah is much more methodical (although she, too, makes an unsubstantiated assertion about the portrait on the cover of her book; in her case it turns out to be true, but we only know this because we have privileged access to the actual events of 1812).

Bernard's approach is inductive reasoning (trying to prove an *a priori* theory) whereas Hannah's is deductive (deducing a theory from evidence). Bernard 'left out everything which doesn't fit' (p. 78); Valentine warns him that his Byron theory is incomplete because it does not take into account the computer analysis of the style of the reviews, but Bernard will not listen. His idea of knowledge is a 'visceral belief' in himself, but for Hannah, nothing less than total proof is good enough; the gaps all have to be filled before one can be absolutely sure of the tune. It is symptomatic that Hannah's predominant discourse mode is to ask questions, whereas Bernard's is to give answers, a difference of style and personality that is particularly noticeable in scenes 2 and 4. Bernard says: 'If knowledge isn't self-knowledge it isn't doing much, mate' (p. 81), yet he seems to suffer from a conspicuous lack of the same. He has no interest in actually being right, only in being seen to be right: 'God, I'm good' (p. 86).

The good news for humanity is that there are occasional breakthroughs, once or twice a century, through luck, perseverance and cooperation; discoveries are still being made that change the world for ever (like man walking on the moon, to use one of Stoppard's examples from another play), and that which was previously believed impossible can be achieved (as Wiles demonstrated by solving Fermat's Last Theorem). The play's general principle seems to be that it is when 'the unpredictable and the predetermined *unfold together*' that new meaning can be created and advances made to the sum of human knowledge.

Fatal knowledge

The play is set in a school room, and all the main characters are seeking some form of intellectual enlightenment. The pursuit of knowledge is presented as a higher good. Septimus says, pompously, but reflecting the view at the time: 'I inspire by reverence for learning and the exaltation of knowledge whereby man may approach God', and nearly 200 years later Hannah says: 'it's the wanting to know that makes

us matter'. However, the acquisition of too much knowledge is traditionally punished in literature by expulsion and/or death; the fanatical pursuit of scientific enquiry frequently ends in madness, as appears to have happened to Septimus, and the mad professor is still a cultural **stereotype**. Although knowledge increases wisdom, it makes one sadder rather than happier (a conceit used in Coleridge's 'The Ancient Mariner' for instance) as it comes with a loss of innocence, and a recognition of life's ephemerality and the inevitability of death.

'Noise'

That knowledge can be elusive is an experience shared by the audience; barriers to the discovery of accurate facts occur in the form of the absence of evidence or data, or the occurrence of unpredictable acts that defeat reasonable supposition, such as when a person annotates another's book, or writes something inherently unlikely (like praise for one's cuckolder), or tells lies about something that is then recorded (like Byron's hare claim), or gives a false impression about how much or what they know, as when Septimus pretends to be giving his own translation of Plutarch. Unattributed and misattributed knowledge are further kinds of 'noise' that distort the pattern, and prejudice also causes academic blindness: Valentine thinks that work on iterated algorithms is only 20 years old and in any case could not possibly have been undertaken by a schoolgirl living in a country house in Derbyshire in eighteen-something. Even Hannah rules out a truth because of bias; being anti-Byron because of her sympathy for Caroline Lamb and because of her resentment at how the 'Byron gang unzipped their flies and patronized all over' her book (p. 29), she states categorically: 'I don't believe [Byron] ever was' at Sidley Park (p. 42). There are numerous occasions on which Bernard shows his contempt for facts or enthusiasm for fictions because of his own preconceived views. Rampant ambition and an over-active imagination are impediments for the true scholar.

Case not proven

Knowledge, says Hannah, 'can't prove to be true, it can only not prove to be false yet' (p. 99). Therefore, one should always keep an open mind. Stoppard has seen enough revisionism in his lifetime, especially concerning the Eastern bloc and the Second World War — which affected him and his family closely — to know that there is no definitive view of history. 'The ultimate fear is of posterity', says Valentine, because of its power to disprove; it does not take long in Bernard's case.

By creating confusion, offering competing theories and leaving some mysteries unsolved, Stoppard seems to be drawing attention to the difficulty in distinguishing fact from fiction or speculation. The knowledge of hindsight is a useful commodity, as the audience realise by knowing more than both the present-day and nineteenth-century characters, but even so we do not know everything. Bernard is wrong to claim that you have to have been there to know what happened, because the play shows us that it does not always help. This is because people lie to each other (e.g. Lady Croom lies in scene 6 about who found Mrs Chater leaving Byron's room), or are too distracted or stupid to notice what is going on, or are too partial to want to accept the truth (such as Chater finding 'the proof of his wife's virtue in his eagerness to defend it', p. 72), so we do not get the full picture. That we can never fully know everything, or perhaps even anything, is fundamental to the human condition, but the desire to try to do so, the wanting to know, is not only what matters but what accounts for human motivation in all areas of life — the spirit of enquiry is what keeps humanity on the road to discovery.

Maths, music and philosophy

Arcadia features two mathematicians, Thomasina Coverly in 1809/1812 and Valentine Coverly in 1993, who are directly related to each other as members of the same family. Septimus is not a mathematician of the same distinction, although he studied Natural Sciences at Cambridge and makes it his life's work, in his incarnation as the hermit after Thomasina's tragic immolation, to attempt to bring her mathematical insights to some conclusion. Valentine, with the benefit of developments in mathematics in the intervening years, and particularly with the invention of computers, is able to do in minutes what Septimus could not do in a lifetime. Maths and physics link concepts schematically in the play:

- mathematics → iterative functions → fractals → Mandelbrot images → nature
- mathematics → Chaos Theory → complexity → population biology → nature
- Newton → irreversibility of phenomena → thermodynamics → entropy → end of the world

Music is an important counterpoint to the theoretical action of *Arcadia*. Although music is an art form, it is the most mathematical one; the intervals between musical notes are composed by precise ratios of frequencies (i.e. proportion, something that is physically apparent in the stopping of the strings of a violin).

The play is also concerned with the fundamental philosophical concepts of **free will** and **determinism**, and the implications for them of the Second Law of Thermodynamics, still in the process of being developed in 1809–12.

Fermat's Theorem

Fermat's Last Theorem is introduced on page 4 of the play as a ridiculously difficult task to distract Thomasina from her uncomfortable line of questioning about 'carnal embrace'. It is also a mystery and, more importantly, introduces a key topic of the play: advanced mathematics. The initial, throwaway reference is reinforced by Septimus's spelling out the theorem on page 4 and introducing equations into the play. In view of Thomasina's later discovery of the properties of iterated functions, it ironically comes to be seen as a much less impossible task for her than might have been supposed. Although it appears that Fermat is not referred to again during the course of the play, this is not in fact true. Thomasina, not at all in awe of the task, states on page 8 'the note in the margin was a joke to make you all mad'. However, that is not the end of the story, because Thomasina subsequently introduces her *New Geometry of Irregular Forms* with a deliberate parody of Fermat: 'This margin being too mean for my purpose' (p. 56). Although Stoppard was presumably unaware of it, as he was writing *Arcadia* the mathematician Andrew Wiles was coming to the end of his 25-year personal odyssey (some of it spent as a 'hermit') to prove Fermat's Last Theorem. The synchronistic relevance of his play appearing as the theorem was finally proved is an effect Stoppard could not have anticipated, thereby providing examples of unpredictability, of history repeating itself and of lost knowledge rediscovered.

Mathematics: science or art?

Mathematics is often thought of as a science. Its practitioners, however, consider it as more akin to philosophy, because it involves rigorously logical thought and conclusions are derived from logical premises known as axioms. But the whole point of fractals and the Mandelbrot set is that they are clearly art and convey an important message about the fundamental relationship of mathematics with both nature and beauty. Hannah says, of Valentine's realisations of members of the Coverley set — inspired by an apple leaf — 'how beautiful!' (p. 100).

Maths and France

The historical background of the Napoleonic era may be reflected in the comments in the play about French and English algebra. Peacock's letter to Thackeray introduces the idea of mathematical rivalry when discussing the hermit's life: 'for it was Frenchified mathematick that brought him to the melancholy certitude of a world without light or life' (p. 87) and that he sought 'the restitution of hope through good English algebra' (ibid.). Hannah picks this up in scene 7: 'From good English algebra?' (p. 103) and Valentine echoes it on the following page. The Second Law of Thermodynamics was developed by several French mathematicians in the early nineteenth century, but it was not English algebra that subverted it; rather, it was Germans who did this with the development of quantum mechanics in the early twentieth century. Peacock (writing in 1862) displays an anti-French prejudice that is not present in Septimus's and Thomasina's discussion of the 'prize essay' (p. 108) in 1812 at the height of the Napoleonic Wars (although Thomasina is disappointed by it being in French). (Note that Stoppard has prepared the ground for this by introducing the discussion in the present-day plot.)

The role of music

Music occurs offstage, but as a necessary background or complement to the main action on stage. The music room adjoins the school room, which is the set for the play and, like the garden that is also never seen, we are constantly aware of it. Thomasina is sent to practise there, which reminds us of the connection between mathematical and musical ability. Gus is musically gifted; he can play the piano through untaught natural talent (p. 63). The waltz in scene 7, which is the culmination of the play, brings all its strands together:

- The waltz is in triple time, the number three in action.
- It brings together romance, art and feeling with the logic, mathematics and science that underlie music.
- It has been suggested that the waltz is a visual analogy of stirring jam into rice pudding.
- The waltz is perhaps the most formal and controlled of all human movements, so negates the effects of chaos.
- However, in its role as the latest London fashion, the waltz symbolises the trivial and ephemeral.
- The waltz survives through time, denying the cruel logic of determinism that everything must end.
- Yet dancing the waltz does lead to the destruction of Thomasina as an individual, and to all the potential and promise that she represents.
- The waltz, typically associated with courtship and love, acts as the vehicle for the actualisation of the love between Thomasina and Septimus that has been bubbling to the surface throughout the play.
- Waltzing together allows Gus and Hannah to show their mutual respect and affection, as well as their empathy with Septimus and Thomasina.

Jam in rice pudding

Thomasina introduces this key concept quite casually on page 6. Her analogy is an example of '**bisociation**', i.e. the linking of disparate fields of knowledge and experience. Septimus immediately points out that time would need to run backwards to reverse the process she describes. She then introduces Newton to allow her to summarise the classical Newtonian position that, with sufficient knowledge of the situation at a particular time, everything that follows could, in principle, be predicted. However, the Second Law of Thermodynamics makes a difference. It is one thing to say that time only runs in one direction and that some actions are irreversible, as Thomasina implies with the rice pudding analogy. According to Newton's laws, many actions are reversible (to every action, there is an equal and opposite reaction); but this theory is undermined by the Second Law of Thermodynamics, which says something else: that you can never get out as much as you put in, that something is always lost. This is what comes to be known as 'entropy', whereby the universe not only inevitably moves from an ordered to a disordered state, but because heat/energy is invariably lost in every transaction, in 'the heat of the smash' (p. 125), so eventually, inevitably, all the energy will be gone and the universe will be still and cold. This is a depressing conclusion, and one that Septimus spends his life as a hermit attempting to 'disprove by good English algebra'.

Trivial pursuits

The play asks questions about what is important and what is trivial: there is a heated discussion between Valentine, Bernard and Hannah in scene 5. Valentine begins by saying 'it's all trivial anyway...who wrote what when' (p. 80). Bernard is outraged, because pursuing and proving authorship is his entire *raison d'être*: 'Why does scientific progress matter more than personalities?' (p. 81) he asks, and concludes, in his customary dismissive style, 'who gives a shit?' (ibid.). Hannah remains silent, but she revisits the idea in scene 7: 'It's wanting to know that makes us matter' (p. 100). This has the ring of Stoppard about it, and Hannah is the character in the play who is given the greatest authority; furthermore, she is allowed the final word on the subject. She admits, with a humility totally contrasting with the bragging of Bernard, to knowing 'Nothing' (p. 128). The play implies that knowledge is itself trivial and ephemeral, and that what actually matters is asking questions, not finding answers.

Arts versus sciences

Hannah and Bernard, at first sight, are the historians and arts scholars. But Septimus teaches literature, Latin (and dancing), and Thomasina despairs at the loss of the Athenian tragedies in the fire of Alexandria. Because the field of fractals and iterated functions falls into both areas, the mathematicians involved (Thomasina and Valentine) cross the divide. Although Septimus, Thomasina and Valentine are the obvious scientists, Chloë also shows an interest, and Hannah is certainly scientific in her approach to evidence, even if it is her instinct that provides the impetus for her ideas. She says: 'Somewhere there will be *something*...if only I can find it' (p. 88), and she does find it in the back of the book on the final page of the play: 'I was looking for that' (p. 130) — the proof that Septimus did become the hermit. Even Ezra Chater is both a poet (mediocre) and a botanist (successful). Bernard, who is too arrogant and egocentric, is not sufficiently scientific: he refuses to exercise proper caution or research methods, and he publishes prematurely on the basis of a hunch, which is rapidly disproved. His reaction 'Am I fucked?' (p. 118) reveals his realisation not that he has failed to live up to the standards of his profession but that he has made a fool of himself. Gus defies any attempt at categorisation. Stoppard specifically wishes to make us think about this blurred and often confused art/science distinction, and to suggest that intelligent and sensitive humans can and should be interested in both, as he himself is; the admirable characters in the play transcend the traditional boundaries between subject areas. 'This is not science. This is story-telling' says Septimus to Thomasina, and the world in general.

Themes and theories

Stoppard has explained that the play's organising principle is the binary opposition between Classicism (represented by Newtonianism) and **Romanticism** (represented by Chaos Theory), and the play therefore fuses two competing frames of reference. The play's **themes** centre around the paradoxes of a predetermined yet unpredictable universe, of a threatened paradise, of a world in which polar opposites, such as art and science, are proved to be similar. The major themes of sex, literature, death and madness are treated elsewhere. Some of the other overall themes operate as binary oppositions: order versus disorder; innocence versus experience; fact versus fiction; truth versus illusion; thinking versus feeling; **comedy** versus **tragedy**; life versus death; heat versus cold.

Time

Time is referred to directly throughout the play, and its structure and plot are predicated upon the passing of time, the creation of history and the concept of coincidence, where two persons or actions share space and/or time. The tortoises are there to represent time, and also as a *memento mori*, since they are a symbol of longevity and typically have a longer lifespan than humans. Although time is scientifically treated as a predictable and absolute concept, Bernard says 'Everything moved more slowly then' (p. 78) and Valentine says 'till there's no time left. That's what time means' (p. 126) to illustrate how we perceive it relatively. Septimus talks, in his set speech on pages 50–51, of life being short and time as both a stealer and a finder of lost knowledge. Time is not reversible: 'You can't run the film backwards', birthdays are a milestone, the earth cannot move from cold to heat, jam in a rice pudding cannot be stirred apart, and 'So we are all doomed'. And yet Stoppard shows time being reversed in the play — doors being built where there are no houses, solved puzzles becoming unsolved again, events happening backwards — in order to play with the paradoxes inherent in the concept of time, and in turning back the clock, or rather going back to the future. Thomasina's age is one of the measurements of the passing of time in the play, and of the changes it brings, one of them being the progression from innocence to experience. Septimus and Thomasina tragically run out of time, as a couple and as individuals.

Mathematics

Thomasina, with her *New Geometry of Irregular Forms*, is the main exponent of maths in the play, supported by Valentine and his grouse population study. Historical mathematicians are referred to throughout, by name or by **allusion**. Some of the technical terms used are of mathematical origin, such as 'trivial' and 'noise'. Computers are a machine to do maths; all they actually do is add and subtract numbers very quickly. Maths stands as a paradigm of logic and **determinism** in opposition to poetry, yet it is nonetheless subject to change and lends itself to being expressed as art; Thomasina draws geometrical objects in scene 7, and Valentine's Coverly set elicits Hannah's awed response to their beauty. Chaos mathematics is the paradigm for human behaviour in the play.

Illusion

In its literal sense of things not appearing as they really are, there are examples of illusion in the play, such as the kiss between Bernard and Hannah, which means nothing more than exuberance. All art is by definition an illusion, and the main use of the concept in the play is an artistic one, whereby designed picturesque landscapes are artfully contrived to appear natural. Supposed evidence can prove illusory and theories can be exploded, whether constructed by Isaac Newton or Bernard Nightingale. The audience is tricked by the illusion of the duel having taken place. Everything we thought we knew can at any time prove to be false, as Valentine points out, and we therefore can be sure of 'Nothing', as Hannah humbly admits.

Unpredictability

On a scientific and human behavioural level much is predictable, and in the **Enlightenment** period it was believed that every aspect of God's creation could be explained and was predetermined. However, **free will** allows sudden, random acts to be performed, like the drawing of the hermit by Thomasina, which have unpredictable consequences, and this is what Chaos Theory is about. Determinism is further incomplete because of 'the attraction that Newton left out', 'the action of bodies in heat' in both meanings of the phrase. The multiple cases of physical attraction that occur in the play, 'fancying people' as Chloë puts it, seem to the audience to be unaccountable in most cases and, since the desire is shown not to be mutual, it is an equation that does not balance and has no laws to explain it. In addition to animal populations, another concept in the play that represents unpredictability is fashion, which dictates much if not all of the behaviour of the first Lady Croom, and, in the form of the waltz, affects Thomasina too.

Iteration

As a maths term, iteration means a self-referential feedback loop, and Thomasina and Valentine are involved in the application of this theory, but there are also other types of repetition in the play. There are verbal echoes between the two eras in the form of names, references, questions, quotations, and whole speeches that call up those of another character. Then there is the iteration of relationships and events and actions, as highlighted in Stoppard's use of **reprise** in the stage directions for the opening of scene 6, and his saying in the opening of scene 3 '*We have seen this composition before*' (p. 46). History repeats itself and time doubles things up; the same beliefs and attitudes come around again, e.g. Hannah's speech on Romanticism in 1993 reiterates that of the first Lady Croom in 1809. 'Once around the garden is not enough'; 'a detail of the previous one blown up' is necessary to be able to establish or recognise the pattern. Multiplicity is fundamental to the play's structure and ideas.

Pattern

Music is a type of pattern, and so is geometry, and pattern is a recurring concept in the play, whether in the visual form of a Mandelbrot fractal image, a design for a landscape or a pair of waltzers. The search for a pattern or order is also applied to the abstract ideas of fate, inevitability and predictability. When patterns are disrupted or pieces are lost, it gets 'very hard to spot the tune', but their emergence is reassuring in an unpredictable world and satisfying to identify, as Valentine appreciates: 'In an ocean of ashes, islands of order. Patterns making themselves out of nothing' (p. 101). Stoppard's plays are highly patterned in their structure, with symmetry, reversals and set pieces, which stand out like 'islands of order' from the confusion of the dialogue.

Sin

Thomasina introduces the theme of sin into the play at the start with the words 'carnal embrace' and her reference to 'the sin of **Onan**' (p. 2). However, it is Septimus and Mrs Chater who have actually already committed a sin by having adulterous carnal knowledge of each other in the garden. The original sin was the eating of the apple by Adam and Eve in the Garden of Eden, which led to lust and banishment, and there are constant reminders of this in the play. In the medieval worldview, wanting to know too much about the workings of the universe was considered an act of transgression against God and a damnable sin, and the debate over the boundaries for permissible human knowledge coloured much Elizabethan literature, such as Marlowe's *Doctor Faustus*. Knowledge was historically denied to women, since it was not only considered unnatural and unnecessary for females to be educated, but it was this very desire to eat the forbidden fruit of the Tree of Knowledge that caused **the Fall**, and all daughters of Eve were blamed. Thomasina's precocious pursuit of knowledge, disapproved of by her mother for social reasons, puts her symbolically at risk of being punished by death for this sin, called **hubris** in Ancient Greece, whose mythology punished humans who overreached themselves.

Images and symbols

Imagery is figurative language, usually **similes** or **metaphors**, which conjures pictures as a means of making memorable both the everyday and the extraordinary, and of forcing **analogies** to be recognised. Imagery can convey **irony** with its double vision, yoking together the actually incongruous but seemingly similar, or vice versa. In addition to reinforcing **themes**, imagery gives atmosphere, pattern, integrity and meaning to a text, and can help to delineate character. This play presents its preoccupations in strongly visual terms, e.g. the landscape books, the geometrical objects, the burning of letters on stage, the waltzing. Chaos mathematics is the overriding and recurring metaphor in the play, as it is an analogy for the unpredictability of human behaviour; the garden is the main **symbol**, and is dealt with elsewhere; jam stirred into rice pudding is the dominant simile, connecting a trivial domestic action with a significant scientific insight into the nature of time and order.

Meat

Images of flesh start on the first page with 'a side of beef' and the Latin '*caro, carnis*'. Caro(line) Lamb's name is a doubly fortuitous one in this connection. Sex and death are linked through both being related to flesh, alive and dead respectively. Rabbits are a byword for sexual activity when alive, and become the components of pies when dead.

Birds

The bird motif is strong, with references to grouse, Turkey, pigeon, Peacock, Nightingale, rooks, and the rest of the list on page 18. The fact that some of them are proper names shows how deliberately and facetiously Stoppard is using bird imagery. The game birds are victims of shooting, the death in the garden. 'Papa has no need of the recording angel, his life is written in the game book' (p. 18).

Noise

The recurring noises exist in the form of the contrasting historical and technological concepts of gunfire, steam engine and piano. In each case the noise causes annoyance to those who have to listen to it, whereas the ideal **Arcadia** is an entirely tranquil place. Noise is also used as a scientific term to mean distracting random data, which prevents the detection of a pattern.

Voyages

The play is a metaphorical voyage of discovery for Hannah, Bernard, Valentine, Septimus, Thomasina — and the audience. The actual voyages (a typically English occupation of travellers, researchers, conquerors and exiles from the sixteenth to the nineteenth centuries, and necessitated by being an island nation) that underpin the play are Byron setting sail for Lisbon and Chater for the West Indies in 1809, one going east and one going west.

Fire

Flames destroy evidence, as when Septimus burns Byron's letter in the spirit lamp. The burning of the library of Alexandria was and still is lamented as the greatest loss to learning and civilisation the world has ever suffered. Thomasina, burned to death the night before her seventeenth birthday, might have had much more knowledge to impart. Septimus's proofs, the work of more than 20 years, were burned on his death. Plutarch's Latin version of the description of Cleopatra in her barge on the Nile includes the phrase '*in igne*', meaning 'on fire'. In the form of gunpowder the use of pistols is literally firing. The fireworks in scene 7 are compared in the stage directions to '*exploding meteors*', once again linking fire with science and destruction. Paradoxically, however, it is when the fire of the sun cools and the earth grows cold, when there is no more energy, that the world will end.

Props as symbols

Rabbits

Septimus shoots a rabbit for Thomasina, to be made into a pie for her, and gives it to Jellaby with blood on it. This could be seen as prefiguring her impending death, especially in conjunction with the interpretation that Septimus is the cause of both deaths. Thomasina gives Septimus an essay with an equation for rabbits eating their own progeny, i.e. life given and then withdrawn, a paradigm of the creation and judgement of man by God.

Apples

The apple presented by Gus to Hannah at the end of scene 2 and the one that Septimus feeds to Plautus in scene 3 are reminiscent of Eve's apple (referred to on p. 97), which is a fundamental image and links to the main themes of the play: knowledge, sin, sex, death, literature, scientific discovery. The apple leaves are the stimulus for thinking for Thomasina and Hannah. As Barton sums it up, the apple is 'an object that gradually comes to symbolise Newton's discovery of the law of gravity, the late-twentieth century geometry of natural forms, the perils of sexuality, any paradise that is lost, and the introduction of death into the world after **the Fall**'.

Game books

Valentine's inheritance is 'A calendar of slaughter', the record of death in the garden and history waiting to be rediscovered in numbers. The game books are the bridge between nature and maths, and an example of dubious written evidence if Byron did not shoot the hare.

Theodolite

The theodolite is in the house and garden and is referred to in the first and last scenes. As a spy glass it is symbolic of the eye of God, and is the cause in both cases of sexual misconduct being found out and punished by expulsion from the garden (Mrs Chater and Bernard respectively): Noakes sees Mrs Chater and Septimus with it, Hannah uses it, and the latter-day Lady Croom is looking for it when she goes to the hermitage and discovers her daughter Chloë with Bernard. As well as being a useful plot device, it is also responsible for Thomasina, who has heard the servants' gossip passed on by Noakes, asking about the meaning of 'carnal embrace' and thus her moving, in Romantic and biblical terms, from innocent childhood to corrupt adulthood. The theodolite crosses the time jump and shows man's continuing fixation with trying to measure nature and control landscape. A pyramid is a symbol of astrological measurement; the theodolite's triangular structure is linked with geometry and the number three as well as with judgement. Though its etymology is obscure, 'theos' is the Greek for 'god'.

Tortoises

Hermits were like tortoises, placed decoratively in the landscape as garden ornaments, and it is therefore fitting that Septimus should feel close to Plautus, be portrayed with him by Thomasina and identified through Peacock's reference to the hermit's companion. Tortoises symbolise longevity (living longer than humans) and therefore time and the re-emergence of lost knowledge.

Pairs

A significant number of props and images occur in twos:

- two garden pictures
- a brace of pistols
- two duel opponents for Septimus
- two waltzing couples
- two letters from Mrs Chater to Hodge
- two tortoises
- two apples
- two apple leaves
- two letters left by Septimus in his room
- Mrs Chater has two husbands, simultaneously in effect
- Bernard believes that there were two Ezra Chaters
- two pairs of hands play the piano in scene 7

Most of the pairings serve the purpose of yoking the two time periods, often ironically. The pairs, which are opposites, remind us of the binary nature of the universe, that a theory can be true or false, the universe hot or cold. Others have a comic effect of excess. Paired images and props are an aspect of the theme of iteration.

Comic devices and fortuitous wit

Stoppardian humour covers a wide spectrum of comic devices from intellectual wit to crude expletives. Though he is better known for his verbal comedy, Stoppard is also fascinated by visual grotesquery and enjoys making his characters look foolish in appearance or putting them in embarrassing, compromising or apparently inexplicable postures or situations that can be misinterpreted by other characters. The main objective of the range of comic devices in this play is the creation of humour through **juxtapositions** that show the collision of worlds. In addition **irony**, **bathos**, inattention, mishearings, misunderstandings, cross purposes, obsessions, interruptions, evasions and slips of the tongue are employed to amusing effect, not only to prove the stupidity of some of the characters but to expose the obstacles to communication.

Puns

The following are examples of words with double meanings used in the play:
- 'noise' used literally as the sense of sound and metaphorically as a scientific term
- 'trivial' as dismissive and as a technical term
- 'irregularity' as moral disapprobation and as a feature of the picturesque style
- 'genius' meaning prodigy and supernatural spirit
- 'oeuvre' meaning collection of a writer's work or main meat dish
- 'Charity' as a character's name and as a virtue
- 'determined' in both its usual and its scientific sense
- 'posing' in its literal and pejorative sense
- 'attraction' in relation to the behaviour of particles and as sexual desire
- 'reckoning' means mathematical calculation and moral judgement
- 'caro' is the diminutive name of Caroline Lamb and the Latin for 'flesh'

These words have different meanings in different contexts, mostly a scientific and an everyday usage. There are additional punning phrases such as 'carnal embrace', 'a bracing experience', 'I demand satisfaction', 'Let him be hanged there for a Lamb', 'who stood up and gave his best', 'the action of bodies in heat'; most of these are *double entendres* that link sex and death. In scene 1 a sustained dialogue at cross purposes is maintained whereby every *double entendre* could relate to both sex and gardening. There are also examples of ambiguity, which add to the potential for offence to be taken and therefore to the humour of the play: 'the photograph doesn't do you justice' (p. 26); 'I spotted something between her legs that made me think of you' (p. 85).

Epigrams

Witty paradoxical utterances abound in the play, e.g. 'As her tutor you have a duty to keep her in ignorance' (p. 15); 'you and Mr Chater shooting each other with the

decorum due to a civilized house' (p. 92); 'A lesson in folly is worth two in wisdom' (p. 13); 'We must have you married before you are educated beyond eligibility' (p. 112). The extended comic exchange on pp. 113–15 between Lady Croom (1) and Noakes is Wildean in character and tone.

Misquotation

Substitutions or reversals of words or phrases create humour by being surprising yet appropriate: 'tock-tick'; 'Brideshead Regurgitated'; 'Culpability Noakes'; 'The Byron gang unzipped their flies and patronized all over it'; 'I often sit with my eyes closed and it doesn't necessarily mean I'm awake'; 'I don't normally like giving credit where it's due'.

Silly words/names

Some words sound humorous regardless of their meaning, just because they are exotic, archaic or childish, e.g. 'gazebo', 'ha-ha', 'Tush', 'Phooey' and 'pooh'. 'Lightning' is wonderfully inappropriate as a name for a tortoise, and Plautus is both an amusing rhyme and relevant name, since Plautus was a comic playwright, Stoppard's Roman equivalent. Jellaby seems to be an example of a Dickensian comic name.

Misunderstandings/mishearings

'Tush' (p. 53) is not only a silly word but it has the added comic advantage of being misunderstood by Brice as a **euphemism** for the female private part, and Septimus believes, or affects to believe, that Thomasina is referring to Fermat's Last Theorem rather than sexual intercourse when she reacts to its description by saying it is 'disgusting and incomprehensible'. The mishearing of 'Etonian' for 'Newtonian' is amusing. There is also the comic device of characters pretending to understand when they actually do not, e.g. Bernard's 'Yes. Why?' and Hannah's 'Oh I see. I don't actually'. (Stoppard has explained this cancelling effect as 'Firstly A, secondly minus A'.) The two kinds of noise are misunderstood. Noakes's inability to understand even when he does hear makes him a comic caricature.

Dysphemism

Examples of crude, rude and taboo language are 'Sod', 'Eat your heart out, you dozy bastards', 'eat shit', 'Piss off', 'who gives a shit?', 'you silly bitch', 'Dickhead', and 'You're fucked'. This is Bernard's speciality in particular, making him seem insensitive, aggressive and arrogant, especially when compared to Hannah, who is the target of most of his offensive utterances. When pushed, however, even she resorts to 'bastard' and 'Bollocks' and 'I'm going to kick you in the balls', which is funny because one does not expect it of her, and it is adolescently incongruous in the context of academic debate.

Stichomythia

This device is much used for comic effect in Stoppard's *Rosencrantz and Guildenstern Are Dead*. It is amusing because of the unrealistic brevity and pace of the exchange of dialogue, which is in effect a battle of wits. The **stichomythia** between Bernard and Hannah on pp. 30–31 and pp. 83–84, between Bernard and Valentine on pp. 23–24 and p. 80, and Septimus and Jellaby on pp. 89–90 conveys the professional or social competitiveness between the pairs of characters.

Alliteration

In context, alliteration can be a mocking and therefore humorous device. There are many examples of it in the speeches of those seeking to ridicule the theories of others by drawing attention to the ludicrous or excessive, and the device is a particular favourite of the first Lady Croom and Bernard. Examples are: 'My hyacinth dell is become a haunt for hobgoblins'; 'waffle on wheels'; 'crystal spheres geared to God's crankshaft'; 'Quarks, quasars — big bangs, black holes'; 'sportive **satyrs** and noodle **nymphs**'; 'Bonking Byron Shot Poet'.

Farce

Unfortunate timings, characters being caught *in flagrante delicto* and sneaking in and out of places are characteristics of farce. It is also ludicrous that Septimus is instructed to communicate with Chater only through Brice when all three are present (p. 52), and the outcome when he attempts to do so is hilarious. Valentine making entrances and immediate exits, and passing across the stage saying 'Sod' over and over again but nothing more (p. 20 and p. 22), are also farcical.

Incongruity

'Bastard', 'bollocks', 'pooh' and 'phooey to death' are unexpected utterances from educated and otherwise respectable characters, which makes such profane language amusing. Chater dying of a monkey bite, having discovered only a 'dwarf' dahlia, is not the expected romantic end for a poet. Bathos derives from incongruous juxtapositions, such as referring to D. H. Lawrence, *Just William* and the *Brighton and Hove Argus* in the same breath. Computer grouse is an **oxymoronic** linkage. As Lady Croom points out to Septimus, talking of rice pudding with jam in one's farewell letter before a duel to the death is not the done thing.

Visual comedy

There are some examples of surreal moments in the play, such as Valentine in Regency dress 'pecking at a portable computer' in scene 7, Septimus stroking the tortoise, and Bernard with his head in a bag/bishop's mitre. The grotesque verbal images of being 'fucked by a dahlia', Chater's *The Maid of Turkey* 'covered in bread sauce and stuffed with chestnuts', and Bernard's universe 'standing on one leg and singing "When father painted the parlour"' also conjure bizarre spectacles.

The tortoises (actually the same but allegedly different) are comic props that seem ridiculously out of place and therefore amusing in their role as paperweights, and Plautus receiving a slice of apple from Septimus is a parody of **the Fall**. Stoppard fans will recognise the intertextual self-reference to *Jumpers* in having a hare/rabbit and a tortoise in this play as well.

Paradox/irony

Stoppard exploits the unlikely and contradictory but ironically true whenever possible, e.g. Septimus's reviews sound more like Byron than Byron's; Thomasina is cleverer than her tutor; Noakes goes to fetch his hat so that he may remove it. It is an amusing **paradox** that one of the proofs of the existence of a hermit at Sidley Park is Thomasina's invention of one as a piece of mischief. It is ironic that 'We're better at predicting events at the edge of the galaxy or inside the nucleus of an atom than whether it will rain on auntie's garden party three Sundays from now', and that Lady Croom (1) regards education as the ruination of a child. Though it is extremely unlikely 'that the man Chater calls his friend Septimus Hodge is the same man who screwed his wife and kicked the shit out of his last book', it is actually true. The fact that grouse were and are bred and protected on country estates specifically in order to be shot provides a background ironic commentary on life and death in the play.

Meiosis and hyperbole

Lady Croom (1) uses this pair of devices to hilarious effect: 'He did not have the manners to mention it' is her reaction to being told by Thomasina that she is going to marry Lord Byron; 'surely a hermit who takes a newspaper is not a hermit in whom one can have complete confidence' ridicules Noakes's suggestion that they advertise the vacancy. She conversely exaggerates that 'snipe and curlew have deserted three counties so that they may be shot in our swamp'. Jellaby's claim that 'The servants are told nothing' when in fact they get to know everything is such an understatement that it becomes the opposite of the truth.

Language and postmodernism

As befits a **postmodernist** work, there are many **genres** and **registers** of language juxtaposed in *Arcadia* (from elevated polite discourse and academic discussion to colloquial banter, including expletives). This is as one would expect in a play that mixes fictional and historical events and characters, and intermingles two historical periods in a complex plot and structure. A parodic revisiting of the past is a common characteristic of postmodernist texts; in addition, Stoppard's play contains the postmodern elements of irregularity, unpredictability, non-linearity, **non sequiturs** and **collage**.

Fiction and non-fiction

Even within the same close context there is a mixing of fiction and non-fiction in the play, e.g. Peacock and Thackeray are both real but James Godolphin is not. Stoppard goes further and inserts fictional material into the published works of non-fictional characters, e.g. Peacock's description of the hermit of Sidley Park. The *DNB* is a real book, but Chater was not a real poet, though of course Byron was, even if his researcher is not. On every level — character, event, reference — the historical is stirred into the imaginary, as inseparably as jam in rice pudding.

Intertextuality and paratextuality

There are numerous **allusions** and references to the titles and contents of works of literature (including the Bible), literary **biography**, scientific works and works of art. Worth particular mention are the two Poussin paintings, one called *Et in Arcadia Ego* and the other *The Arcadian Shepherds* (see p. 25). Inserted throughout the play are quotations, genuine and fictional. Count Zelinsky is a fictional character in an anonymous novel of 1840 called *The Female Freemasons*, itself a paradoxical concept. See *Historical characters* on pp. 100–04 for the numerous famous names, in the fields of science and art, that are mentioned in the play. Diagrams and sketches link to the verbal subject matter; Sidley Park garden, hermits, geometrical solids, leaves, heat exchange, Caroline Lamb and Byron, Septimus and Plautus are all drawn as well as described and discussed, and fractal imagery is maths turned into an art form.

Registers and genres

Many areas of study lend terminology to the play: maths (theorem, iteration, algorithm, calculus, geometry); physics (thermodynamics, heat exchange, steam engine, relativity, quantum); biology/botany (population change, manipulation, dwarf dahlia); computing (feedback, noise, trivia); literature (**oxymoron**, oeuvre, **epiphany**, rhetoric); gardening (ha-ha, gazebo, hermitage, steam pump, dell, propagate, game book). The range of technical terms gives linguistic reinforcement to the thematic idea of cross-disciplines and the **characterisation** of Septimus and Thomasina as polymaths. Many of the above terms belong in more than one category of human activity. The amalgam of language and languages (French and Latin) gives a rich and potentially comic texture to the **diction**, enabling misunderstandings and multiplicity of meanings to occur, e.g. 'caro' is Latin for flesh and 'canard' is French for duck, yet another bird.

The main form of written text is the letter in all its forms: personal and impersonal, private and published, signed and anonymous. In addition, there is at least one of each of the following: literary lecture, magazine article, letter to a newpaper editor, Latin prose, billet-doux, game book entry, news headline, poem extract, Latin tag, maths theorem, physical law, dedication, travel writing passage, essay title, gardening book extract. The collage of genres gives variety and intellectual liveliness to the text, allowing different voices and viewpoints to be heard, from different time periods, in addition to those of the characters, and introducing other events from outside the time and setting of the play. The inconsistency of genre militates against a homogenous style and register, creating a mood of transience and absence of predictability relevant to the play's **themes**. In addition, the style of utterance of 1809/1812 is clearly distinct in its vocabulary and syntax from the modern style of speech, showing how change has also occurred in the English language, e.g. the archaisms 'Pray', 'pianoforte' and 'I keep my room this day'.

Creating uncertainty

The postmodernist writer aims to shock, obfuscate and undermine audience expectation. Act I ends with the sound of a gunshot, which is apparently the duel but turns out to have been the shooting of a rabbit. It is a shock to discover later on that 'the girl who died in the fire' must be Thomasina. The play ends symmetrically but denies the audience closure in that we know this is not really an end: the loose ends are not tied up and we are not clear what is about to happen. Typically there is an avoidance of feeling and psychological interpretation in postmodernist works; no one's behaviour is explained in this play, though some of it deserves to be, given the unconventional or extreme actions, e.g. that of Mrs Chater, Septimus, Lady Croom (1) and Gus. Uncertainty is the main feeling the audience experience, and it is also that of many of the characters.

Set speeches

It is Stoppard's trademark to include one or more passionate monologues in each of his plays, in which a key character (and often one not otherwise moved to express his/her feelings) gets to the heart of the matter and delivers an intellectual appeal that relates to an essential **theme** and includes the play's recurring **imagery**. Characteristically these set speeches consist of very short or non-sentences, as if to emulate the thought process of a mind deeply engaged and struggling for the suitably forceful and succinct expression of a complex and important idea.

Septimus pp. 50–51

By counting our stock. Seven plays from Aeschylus, seven from Sophocles, *nineteen* from Euripides, my lady! You should no more grieve for the rest than for a buckle lost from your first shoe, or for your lesson book which will be lost when you are old. We shed as we pick up, like travellers who must carry everything in their arms, and what we let fall will be picked up by those behind. The procession is very long and life is very short. We die on the march. But there is nothing outside the march so nothing can be lost to it. The missing plays of Sophocles will turn up piece by piece, or be written again in another language. Ancient cures for diseases will reveal themselves once more. Mathematical discoveries glimpsed and lost to view will have their time again. You do not suppose, my lady, that if all of Archimedes had been hiding in the great library of Alexandria, we would be at a loss for a corkscrew? I have no doubt that the improved steam-driven heat-engine which puts Mr Noakes into an ecstasy that he and it and the modern age should all coincide, was described on papyrus. Steam and brass were not invented in Glasgow...

Septimus does not normally say anything that reveals personal sentiment, nor does he speak in utterances longer than one line, his normal mode being caustic and urbane. He is therefore assumed to feel strongly about this subject, and possibly to feel strongly about Thomasina, since he takes such pains to reassure her that she should not grieve for lost knowledge. The sustained **metaphor** of the journey of life gives the passage its integrity. **Irony** is present, since Thomasina's lesson book was not lost, which raises a doubt as to whether Septimus is also wrong about the other claims he is making here, though the plot of the play justifies his assertion that those behind will pick up what is dropped, as Valentine, Gus, Hannah and Bernard do. The extra-fictional proof of the shedding and redis-covery theory is that Fermat's Last Theorem was finally and fortuitously solved after this speech was written, and it is a fact that Leonardo da Vinci did drawings of helicopters, a twentieth-century invention. The question and exclamation marks betray passion and reveal a hidden side to Thomasina's tutor.

Lady Croom pp. 15–16

Your drawing is a very wonderful transformation. I would not have recognized my own garden but for your ingenious book — is it not? — look! Here is the Park as it appears to us now, and here as it might be when Mr Noakes has done with it. Where there is the familiar pastoral refinement of an Englishman's garden, here is an eruption of gloomy forest and towering crag, of ruins where there was never a house, of water dashing against rocks where there was neither spring nor a stone I could not throw the length of a cricket pitch. My hyacinth dell is become a haunt for hobgoblins, my Chinese bridge, which I am assured is superior to the one at Kew, and for all I know at Peking, is usurped by a fallen obelisk overgrown with briars —

This is an amusing satire on the excesses of the **Gothic** picturesque style as Romantic replaces classical landscape in English country estates, and the pleasing and attractive gives way to the macabre and threatening. Hannah gives a **reprise** of these views when she attacks the whole 'Romantic sham'. The before and after effect, symbolised in the sketch book, is what is captured in the play as a whole by the alternating time periods. The emphasis on the subject pronouns 'I' and 'me' convey the egocentricity and assertiveness of Lady Croom's character, and the content on her diatribe and attack on the hapless Noakes reveals her delight in her garden and in her position as a leader of fashion.

Valentine p. 62

If you knew the algorithm and fed it back say ten thousand times, each time there'd be a dot somewhere on the screen. You'd never know where to expect the next dot. But gradually you'd start to see this shape, because every dot will be inside the shape of this leaf. It wouldn't *be* a leaf, it would be a mathematical object. But yes. The unpredictable and the predetermined unfold together to make everything the way it is. It's how nature creates itself, on every scale, the snowflake and the snowstorm. It makes me so happy. To be at the beginning again, knowing almost nothing. People were talking about the end of physics. Relativity and quantum looked as if they were going to clean out the whole problem between them. A theory of everything. But they only explained the very big and the very small. The universe, the elementary particles. The ordinary-sized stuff which is our lives, the things people write poetry about — clouds — daffodils — waterfalls — and what happens in a cup of coffee when the cream goes in — these things are full of mystery, as mysterious to us as the heavens were to the Greeks. We're better at predicting events at the edge of the galaxy or inside the nucleus of an atom than whether it'll rain on auntie's garden party three Sundays from now. Because the problem turns out to be different. We can't even predict the next drip from a dripping tap when it gets irregular. Each drip sets up the conditions for the next, the smallest variation blows prediction apart, and the weather is unpredictable the same way, will always be unpredictable. When you push the numbers through the computer you can see it on the screen. The future is disorder. A door like this has cracked open five or six times since we got up on our hind legs. It's the best possible time to be alive, when almost everything you thought you knew is wrong.

Valentine is in his own head and world, playing the role of the stereotypical scientist immersed in and excited by his work, so he is not really talking to Hannah. His expression is noticeably lacking in fluidity and complexity of syntax, as if he finds such a long speech taxing and is normally a thinker rather than a talker. There is a use of imagery and example, however, which shows that he has an artistic streak and a sense of humour. What he is saying is directly relevant to the themes of knowledge, discovery, predictability, nature and Chaos Theory, and links him to Thomasina. His references to the mystery of natural features that occur in Romantic poetry — cloud, daffodils, waterfalls — and his resistance to the idea that we should have a 'theory of everything' make him a Romantic at heart, despite being a research scientist.

Hannah p. 100

Oh, that. It's *all* trivial — your grouse, my hermit, Bernard's Byron. Comparing what we're looking for misses the point. It's wanting to know that makes us matter. Otherwise we're going out the way we came in. That's why you can't believe in the afterlife, Valentine. Believe in the after, by all means, but not the life. Believe in God, the soul, the spirit, the infinite, believe in angels if you like, but not in the great celestial get-together for an exchange of views. If the answers are in the back of the book I can wait, but what a drag. Better to struggle on knowing that failure is final.

Ignorance is unacceptable in Hannah's philosophy, and in her view there are no limits to the questions that may be asked, that should be asked, if the purpose of humanity is to be fulfilled. There is a directness of thought and expression in this speech that conveys Hannah's honest approach to the acquisition of knowledge and the adoption of belief. Unlike Bernard, she is not afraid of failure. The struggle of enquiry is what keeps her mind alive and engaged, and is more interesting to her than the answers; she is a latter-day Thomasina in this way. She keeps an open mind and learns fast, as shown by her having taken on board the maths term 'trivial'. This speech shows a rare insight into Hannah's fundamentally responsive but carefully controlled personality.

Bernard pp. 81–82

Oh, you're going to zap me with penicillin and pesticides. Spare me that and I'll spare you the bomb and aerosols. But don't confuse progress with perfectibility. A great poet is always timely. A great philosopher is an urgent need. There's no rush for Isaac Newton. We were quite happy with Aristotle's cosmos. Personally, I preferred it. Fifty-five crystal spheres geared to God's crankshaft is my idea of a satisfying universe. I can't think of anything more trivial than the speed of light. Quarks, quasars — big bangs, black holes — who gives a shit? How did you people con us out of all that status? All that money? And why are you so pleased with yourselves? […] I'd push the lot of you over a cliff myself. Except the one in the wheelchair, I think I'd lose the sympathy vote before people had time to think it through. […] If knowledge isn't self-knowledge it isn't doing much, mate. Is the universe expanding? Is it contracting? Is it standing on one leg and singing 'When Father Painted the Parlour'? Leave me out. I can expand my universe without you. 'She walks in beauty, like the night of cloudless climes and starry skies, and all that's best of dark and bright meet in her aspect and her eyes.' There you are, he wrote it after coming home from a party…

Bernard is obviously an experienced public speaker and demander of attention. There are a number of phrases balanced by 'and' in this speech, and the alliteration is striking, as is the use of rhetorical questions. On the other hand, he descends to the colloquial and even lower, with offensive and provocative **diction** (such as 'mate' and 'the other one in the wheelchair'). His **tone** is not only dogmatic but aggressive. The art/science dichotomy is one that obviously bothers Bernard a lot because of its social and financial impact. It is perhaps surprising that he holds Byron's poetry in such reverence, which is evidence that characters in this play have a carapace or can be more complex than they appear. Nonetheless, Bernard does not manage to win 'the sympathy vote'.

Hannah p. 36

The whole Romantic sham, Bernard! It's what happened to the Enlightenment, isn't it? A century of intellectual rigour turned in on itself. A mind in chaos suspected of genius. In a setting of cheap thrills and false emotion. The history of the garden says it all, beautifully. There's an engraving of Sidley Park in

1730 that makes you want to weep. Paradise in the age of reason. By 1760 everything had gone — the topiary, pools and terraces, fountains, an avenue of limes — the whole sublime geometry was ploughed under by Capability Brown. The grass went from the doorstep to the horizon and the best box hedge in Derbyshire was dug up for the ha-ha so that the fools could pretend they were living in God's countryside. And then Richard Noakes came in to bring God up to date. By the time he'd finished it looked like this (*the sketch book*). The decline from thinking to feeling, you see.

Hannah is putting the case for the **Enlightenment** versus **Romanticism** in this speech. She mentions several of the play's keywords: genius, chaos, Paradise, geometry. For her the destruction of the garden symbolises change and decay and 'says it all'.

Thomasina p. 49

You are churlish with me because mama is paying attention to your friend. Well, let them elope, they cannot turn back the advancement of knowledge. I think it is an excellent discovery. Each week I plot your equations dot for dot, *x*s against *y*s in all manner of algebraical relation, and every week they draw themselves as commonplace geometry, as if the world of forms were nothing but arcs and angles. God's truth, Septimus, if there is an equation for a curve like a bell, there must be an equation for one like a bluebell, and if a bluebell, why not a rose? Do we believe nature is written in numbers?

Thomasina is perceptive and can read Septimus; she is aware that he is jealous of Byron and desirous of her mother. She is making the point that the march of knowledge cannot be stopped by any personal or historical event. Mathematical numbers and nature's numbers are brought together through the **bisociation** of the bell curve and the bluebell. She is leading the discussion, showing confidence in her abilities and asserting her personality in an adult world. It is clear that by this stage she has already become the dominant partner in the teacher/pupil relationship and is no longer dependent on Septimus for her understanding of either emotions or maths.

Critical comments

The critical history of this play has centred on **epistemological** issues and processes and has particularly attracted German scholars. The contention is mainly how seriously Stoppard is claiming that the truth will out, that the lost can be refound and that history can be accurately reconstructed. There is further argument about whether the misunderstandings in the play obfuscate or reveal, and therefore whether they are creative or destructive. The pros argue that Hannah arrives at the truth and it is her process that works; the antis argue that it is purely fortuitous that Gus fancies her — the unpredictability of attraction — and therefore finds her proof, and that the general trend of the play is towards uncertainty as a principle. The other debate concerns the fact that knowledge is equated with sin in the context of Adam and Eve being punished in the Garden of Eden for eating the forbidden fruit of the Tree of Knowledge, and that therefore 'wanting to know' may be being presented as a dubious and dangerous pursuit for humanity, since it is punishable by death, as illustrated by the killing of Thomasina.

Using critical comments in exam and coursework essays shows wider reading, an appreciation of other readers' views, an ability to support one's own view and an understanding of the techniques, aims and **themes** of Stoppard's writing in general, and of this play in particular. Below are lists of comments made by Ronald Hayman and other critics on Stoppard and *Arcadia*.

Ronald Hayman on Stoppard

- [Stoppard's plays] are not so much drama as audio-visual metaphysics.
- He strings characters like puppets on a line of **repartee**.
- [His plays] spin off like eccentric Catherine wheels. [They are] firework displays of verbal ingenuity.
- We, the audience, are having a moral experience because we are watching a group of people who are not.
- [His plays have] uproarious comedy with unsettling undercurrents.
- [Stoppard writes] plays of ideas uneasily married to **comedy** or **farce**.
- Metaphysical unease […] is Stoppard's trademark.
- [Stoppard's subject matter is] the discontinuity between the human condition and the human imagination.
- [Stoppard tackles] the fear of living in an impossible universe.
- [Stoppard has] a fascination with the interconnectedness between then and now, the unreliability of evidence, the haphazardness of what survives.
- [Stoppard is a] creative nihilist.
- Nothing in the play is purely arbitrary, nothing is there just for a quick laugh.
- Stoppard is a mixture of mathematician, engineer, entertainer and surrealist.
- [Stoppard enjoys] folding things back on themselves so that they get thicker.

Other critics on Stoppard

- [Stoppard's works contain] endless leapfrogging reversals. (*Irving Wardle*, Independent on Sunday, *28 March 1993*)
- Stoppard has always delighted in arcane **analogies** and incongruous congruities. (*Benedict Nightingale*, The Times, *15 April 1993*)

Comments on *Arcadia*

- [The play] seldom relaxes its comic grip or its narrative tension. [*ibid.*]
- The play is Stoppard's tribute to the complexity, unpredictability and inscrutability of the world — pet themes since *Rosencrantz and Guildenstern Are Dead* — and he pays it with style and cunning. [*ibid.*]

- [It is] a play always pulling slyly satisfactory surprises. [*ibid.*]
- *Arcadia* constantly engages the imaginary in a dialogue with the historically true. (*Anne Barton, 1995*)

Stoppard's comments on his work

- **Parody** is positively lethal: it makes you think and laugh at the same time.
- Extreme seriousness co-exists happily with extreme frivolity.
- My distinguishing mark is an absolute lack of certainty about almost anything.
- I write plays because **dialogue** is the most respectable way of contradicting myself.
- **Biography** is the mesh through which our real life escapes.
- Things are so interrelated.
- My plays are convergences of different threads.
- Dislocation of an audience's assumptions is an important part of what I like to write.
- My characters are all mouthpieces for points of view [...]. They aren't realistic in any sense.

Essential quotations

The best quotations to know are those you have found useful in class discussions and practice essays, and they will require little conscious learning because you are already familiar with them. The most effective ones to learn in addition are those that serve more than one purpose, i.e. that can be used to support a **theme**, image or style usage as well as a point about character or dramatic effect.

Act I

Scene 1

- Carnal embrace is the practice of throwing one's arms around a side of beef. (*Septimus to Thomasina*)
- ...in the scheme of the garden he is as the serpent. (*Septimus to Thomasina about Noakes*)
- You cannot stir things apart. (*Thomasina to Septimus about irreversibility of time*)
- Am I the first person to have thought of this? (*Thomasina to Septimus about determinism*)
- A lesson in folly is worth two in wisdom. (*Lady Croom about Thomasina*)
- ...it is nature as God intended, and I can say with the painter, 'Et in Arcadia ego!' 'Here I am in Arcadia,' Thomasina. (*Lady Croom about the present garden at Sidley Park*)
- *The Castle of Otranto* was written by whomsoever I say it was, otherwise what is the point of being a guest or having one? (*Lady Croom to Mr Chater*)
- A calendar of slaughter. 'Even in Arcadia, there am I!' (*Septimus to Thomasina*)
- Oh, phooey to Death! (*Thomasina*)
- You must not be cleverer than your elders. It is not polite. (*Septimus to Thomasina*)

Scene 2

- *A peacock-coloured display handkerchief boils over in his breast pocket. (stage direction describing Bernard)*
- *Gus doesn't speak. He never speaks. Perhaps he cannot speak. (stage direction describing Gus)*
- English landscape was invented by gardeners imitating foreign painters who were evoking classical authors. (*Hannah to Bernard*)
- The history of the garden says it all, beautifully. (*Hannah to Bernard*)
- And then Richard Noakes came in to bring God up to date…The decline from thinking to feeling, you see. (*Hannah to Bernard about Romanticism*)

Scene 3

- We shed as we pick up…and what we let fall will be picked up by those behind. (*Septimus to Thomasina about loss of knowledge*)
- If that was not God speaking through Lady Croom, he never spoke through anyone! (*Brice about his sister*)

Scene 4

- The unpredictable and the predetermined unfold together to make everything the way it is. (*Valentine to Hannah*)
- The future is disorder. (*Valentine to Hannah*)
- Tock, tick goes the universe and then recovers itself, but it was enough, you were in there and you bloody *know*. (*Bernard to Hannah about instinct*)

Act II

Scene 5

- …the drama of life and death at Sidley Park was not about pigeons but about sex and literature. (*Bernard reading his lecture for the Byron Society to Hannah, Valentine, Chloë and Gus*)
- …it was the woman who bade me eat. (*Bernard pretending to quote Byron quoting Milton paraphrasing Genesis*)
- You've left out everything which doesn't fit. (*Hannah to Bernard about his theory*)
- Caroline was Romantic waffle on wheels with no talent, and Byron was an eighteenth-century Rationalist touched by genius. (*Bernard to Hannah*)
- It takes a romantic to make a heroine of Caroline Lamb. You were cut out for Byron. (*Bernard to Hannah*)

Scene 6

- It has been a night of reckoning. (*Septimus to Lady Croom about banishing the Chaters and Byron*)

Scene 7

- 'Even in Arcadia — Sex, Literature and Death at Sidley Park' (*title of newspaper article about Bernard's theory*)
- The attraction that Newton left out. All the way back to the apple in the garden. (*Valentine to Chloë about sex*)
- The ultimate fear is of posterity… (*Valentine to Hannah*)
- It's wanting to know that makes us matter. (*Hannah to Valentine*)
- In an ocean of ashes, islands of order. (*Valentine to Hannah about Mandelbrot sets*)
- *Septimus and Hannah turn the pages, doubled by time.* (*stage direction*)
- …there's an order things can't happen in. You can't open a door till there's a house. (*Valentine to Hannah about discovery*)
- The bright sun was extinguished…and the icy earth / Swung blind and blackening in the moonless air… (*Hannah quoting from Byron's poem 'Darkness'*)
- The Chater would overthrow the Newtonian system in a weekend. (*Thomasina to herself about sexual attraction*)
- It will make me mad as you promised. (*Septimus to Thomasina about the Second Law of Thermodynamics*)
- So, we are all doomed. (*Septimus to Thomasina (and Valentine) about heat exchange*)
- This is not science. This is story-telling. (*Septimus to Thomasina about heat exchange*)
- …you can't run the film backwards. (*Valentine to Hannah*)
- When we have found all the mysteries and lost all the meaning, we will be alone, on an empty shore. (*Septimus to Valentine*)

Historical characters

Aeschylus (525 BC–456 BC) Ancient Greek tragedian

Alexander the Great (356 BC–323 BC) King of Macedon and conqueror of most of the known world; he probably died as a result of a mosquito bite

Alexander (1893–1920) king of Greece; died as a result of a monkey bite

Archimedes (c. 287 BC–c. 212 BC) Ancient Greek mathematician; famous for saying '*Eureka!*'

Aristotle (384 BC–322 BC) Ancient Greek philosopher

Charles Babbage (1791–1871) English mathematician who originated the idea of a programmable computer

Sir Joseph Banks (1743–1820) botanist, explorer, president of the Royal Society; corresponded with Carl Linnaeus

William Blake (1757–1827) Romantic poet, best known for *Songs of Innocence and of Experience*

Napoleon Bonaparte (1769–1821) Revolutionary emperor of France during the Napoleonic Wars

Lancelot 'Capability' Brown (1716–83) best known of a group of eighteenth-century landscape architects who rejected the formalism of Italian and French garden design for an idealised 'asymmetric' natural pastoral landscape derived from the paintings of Claude and Poussin

'Beau' Brummel (1778–1840) celebrated 'dandy'; arbiter of fashion in Regency London

Lord Byron (1788–1824) Romantic poet; celebrated womaniser who left England and died in Greece during the war of independence against the Turks

Nicolas Sadi Carnot (1796–1832) mathematician who developed the heat engine and had early insights into the Second Law of Thermodynamics

Lewis Carroll (1832–98) *nom de plume* of Charles Lutwidge Dodgson, Oxford mathematician and author of *Alice's Adventures in Wonderland*

Thomas Chippendale (1718–79) celebrated designer of furniture

Claude (Lorrain) (1600–82) French landscape painter whose work was used as a model by eighteenth-century landscape gardeners

Rudolf Clausius (1822–88) German physicist who introduced the concept of entropy

Cleopatra (69 BC–30 BC) queen of Egypt; central character in Shakespeare's *Antony and Cleopatra*; legend has it that she died from a snake bite

Samuel Taylor Coleridge (1772–1834) Romantic poet, known for his epic poem 'The Ancient Mariner'

Dido (*c.* ninth century BC) legendary queen of Carthage who died by throwing herself on a fire when abandoned by her lover, Aeneas, in Virgil's *Aeneid*

Arthur Eddington (1882–1944) British astronomer who coined the term 'Arrow of Time'

Albert Einstein (1879–1955) German Jewish mathematician who fled to the USA to avoid persecution by the Nazis; inventor of relativity

Euclid (active *c.* 300 BC) Ancient Greek mathematician, 'the Father of Geometry'

Euripides (*c.* 480 BC–406 BC) Ancient Greek tragedian

Pierre de Fermat (1601–65) French mathematician whose 'Last Theorem' was not proven until 1994

Baron Jean-Joseph Fourier (1768–1830) French mathematician who developed a 'Heat Equation'

Henry Fuseli (1741–1825) Swiss-born British painter best known for his Gothic style

Galileo Galilei (1564–1642) Italian astronomer and physicist who played an important role in the Scientific Revolution

Johann Wolfgang von Goethe (1749–1832) German Romantic poet

'Guercino' (1591–1666) (really Giovanni Francesco Barbieri) Italian painter who painted the original *Et in Arcadia Ego*

John Hanson Byron's solicitor, to whom he wrote before leaving England suddenly in 1809

Stephen Hawking (b. 1942) wheelchair-bound British physicist, best known for *A Brief History of Time*

Werner Heisenberg (1901–76) brilliant German physicist; one of the founders of quantum mechanics who developed the Uncertainty Principle

Hermann von Helmholtz (1821–94) German mathematician who wrote a treatise on the conservation of energy

Thomas Hobbes (1588–1679) British political philosopher, best known for *Leviathan*

Lady Holland (Elizabeth Fox) (1770–1845) brought first dahlias to England from Spain in 1804

Francis Jeffrey (1773–1850) Scottish literary critic and editor of the *Edinburgh Review*

John the Baptist (first century BC) Jewish prophet who was, according to the Bible, beheaded on the orders of Salome; his head was presented to her on a silver salver

Dr (Samuel) Johnson (1709–84) a major Augustan literary figure famous for his wit; author of the first English dictionary

William Kent (*c.* 1685–1748) pioneer English landscape gardener who created 'Arcadian' gardens for country houses

Lady Caroline Lamb (1785–1828) aristocrat and novelist, achieved notoriety for her adulterous affair with Byron

D. H. Lawrence (1885–1930) controversial English novelist who included explicit erotic content

Gottfried Leibnitz (1646–1716) German philosopher and mathematician who discovered calculus independently of Newton

Carl Linnaeus (1707–78) Swedish botanist; one of the pioneers of the classification of species

Ada Lovelace (1815–52) Byron's only legitimate child, a maths prodigy and collaborator with Charles Babbage

René Magritte (1898–1967) Belgian surrealist painter

Benoît Mandelbrot (b. 1924) Polish-French mathematician, best known for his 'Mandelbrot set' of fractals

James Clerk Maxwell (1831–79) mathematician and physicist

John Milton (1608–74) celebrated English poet, author of *Paradise Lost*, which tells the story of the Fall

Thomas Moore (1779–1852) Irish poet who nearly fought a duel with Francis Jeffrey over a hostile review in the *Edinburgh Review* in 1806

John Murray (1778–1843) Byron's friend and publisher

Thomas Newcomen (1663–1729) inventor in 1712 of the steam engine and steam pump

Sir Isaac Newton (1642–1727) renowned British physicist and astronomer, best known for inventing the Theory of Gravity

Florence Nightingale (1820–1910) pioneer of modern nursing techniques in the Crimean War

Ovid (43 BC–AD 17) notable Roman poet who wrote odes about Arcadia

Thomas Love Peacock (1785–1866) English novelist and writer; mainly associated with Gothic novels

Pericles (*c.* 495 BC–429 BC) leading statesman in classical Athens

Plato (428 BC–348 BC) Ancient Greek philosopher

Plautus (born *c.* 254 BC) Roman comic playwright

Plutarch (*c.* AD 46–127) Ancient Greek historian; his *Lives* was an important source for Shakespeare

Siméon Denis Poisson (1781–1840) French mathematician who developed the work of Fourier

Alexander Pope (1688–1744) Augustan poet who had a grotto in his garden at Twickenham

Nicolas Poussin (1594–1665) French painter who painted the most celebrated version of *Et in Arcadia Ego*

Ptolemy (*c.* AD 90–168) celebrated Ancient Egyptian mathematician and astronomer

Mrs (Ann) Radcliffe (1764–1823) pioneer author of Gothic novels

Humphry Repton (1752–1818) leading English landscape gardener who created a 'Red Book' for each garden (named for their red morocco bindings), which included watercolours of prospects after 'improvement', with flaps showing 'before'

Samuel Rogers (1763–1855) a minor poet who was a friend of Byron

Salvator Rosa (1615–73) Italian landscape painter of wild and brooding scenes

Jean-Jacques Rousseau (1712–78) Enlightenment philosopher from Geneva who stressed the importance of nature

Jacopo Sannazzaro (1458–1530) Italian writer best known for writing *Arcadia* (published 1504)

Erwin Schrödinger (1887–1961) Austrian physicist who was a pioneer of quantum mechanics, famous for his proposed 'cat experiment' (1935)

Sir Walter Scott (1771–1832) Scottish novelist who wrote reviews for the *Edinburgh Review*

Mary Shelley (1797–1851) writer of *Frankenstein* (published 1818); wife of Byron's fellow poet

Simon Singh (b. 1964) Punjabi-English writer who wrote *Fermat's Last Theorem*

Sophocles (*c.* 496 BC–406 BC) Ancient Greek tragedian

Robert Southey (1774–1843) English Romantic poet and Poet Laureate (1813–43)

William Robert Spencer (1769–1834) minor English poet

W. M. Thackeray (1811–63) English novelist and editor of the *Cornhill Magazine*

Virgil (70 BC–19 BC) Roman poet who originally romanticised Arcadia in his *Eclogues*; wrote the epic *Aeneid*

Horace Walpole (1717–97) author of Gothic novel *The Castle of Otranto*; advocate of Gothic style in landscape and architecture

Hugh Walpole (1884–1941) English novelist

Oscar Wilde (1854–1900) Anglo-Irish comic playwright, best known for *The Importance of Being Earnest* (1895) and his epigrammatic style

Andrew Wiles (b. 1953) English mathematician who proved Fermat's Last Theorem

William Wordsworth (1770–1850) English Romantic poet and Poet Laureate (1843–50)

Literary terms and concepts

The terms and concepts below have been selected for their relevance to talking and writing about *Arcadia*. It will aid argument and expression to become familiar with them and to use them in your discussion and essays.

acte gratuit	gratuitous impulsive act
allegory	extended metaphor that veils a moral or political underlying meaning, e.g. a garden representing Paradise
allusion	passing reference to another literary work, without naming it
ambiguity	capacity of words to have two simultaneous meanings in the same context
anachronism	chronological misplacing of person, event or object
analogy	perception of similarity between two things
anecdote	a brief written or spoken account of an amusing incident, often used to illustrate a point
antithesis	contrasting of ideas by balancing words or phrases of opposite meaning
Antony and Cleopatra	Shakespeare's tragedy exemplifying personal and political catastrophe caused by sexual attraction
Apocalypse	Greek for 'revelation'; biblical name for the end of the world by fire
Arcadia	a rural area of peace, simplicity and fertility used in literature to represent an idyllic life among shepherds; located in southern Greece
archaism	grammar or **diction** not in common use at time of writing
archetype	original model used as recurrent **symbol**, e.g. serpent as evil
ars longa vita brevis	Latin translation of words by the Greek Hippocrates; often misunderstood, it means that although life is short, it takes a long time to acquire a craft or skill

bathos	descent from the sublime to the ridiculous (Septimus accuses Chater of having reduced love to bathos with his 'sportive **satyrs** and noodle **nymphs**')
biography	account of an individual's life written by someone else
bisociation	Koestler's term in *Act of Creation* (1964) for innovative thinking, leading to discoveries, caused by linking two fields not previously associated
black comedy	treating serious or painful subjects, e.g. death, as amusing
bon mot	a clever word or witticism
caricature	exaggerated and ridiculous portrayal of a person built around a specific physical or personality trait, e.g. Noakes's bewilderment
carpe diem	Latin tag meaning 'seize the opportunity'; a Romantic tenet
characterisation	means by which fictional characters are personified and made distinctive
classical	eighteenth-century artistic movement deriving its inspiration from Ancient Greece and Rome; restrained and formal style
cliché	predictable and overused expression or situation
climax	moment of intensity to which a series of events has been leading
collage	'pasting' together of texts belonging to different **genres** and **registers**; typical of **postmodernist** texts
colloquial	informal language of conversational speech
comedy	Ancient Greek form of drama in which confusions and deceptions are unravelled, with amusement along the way, ending in resolution, restitution and reconciliation
connotation	association evoked by a word, e.g. waltzing connotes romance
contextuality	historical, social and cultural background of a text
criticism	evaluation of literary text or other artistic work
determinism	the theory that human beings are not free agents, but that their actions are governed by external causes and therefore, in principle, predictable
dialogue	direct speech of characters engaged in conversation
diction	choice of words; vocabulary from a particular semantic field, e.g. mathematics
dictum	a noteworthy or authoritative statement
Don Juan	a legendary fictional libertine, originating in fourteenth-century Spain; one of Byron's most celebrated poems

double entendre	expression with two meanings, one of them coarse
drama	composition in verse or prose, involving conflict, which is performed through action and **dialogue**
dramatic irony	when the audience know something that the character speaking does not, which creates humour or tension
dysphemism	deliberate use of crude or taboo language for startling effect; opposite of **euphemism**; Bernard's **idiolect**
eclogue	type of **pastoral** verse normally in the form of a monologue or dialogue between shepherds. Virgil's *Eclogues* are set in Arcadia
elegy	lament for the death or permanent loss of someone or something
empathy	identifying with a character in a literary work
Enlightenment	philosophical movement of the eighteenth century that emphasised rationality, scientific thought and human rights; it led to the rise of democracy and contributed to the French and American Revolutions
epigram	short, concise, original and witty saying, often including rhyme, alliteration, assonance or antithesis; associated with Oscar Wilde
epiphany	sudden and striking revelation of the essence of something sublime; realisation that 'everything you thought you knew is wrong'
epistemology	branch of philosophy that studies the nature, methods, limitations and validity of knowledge and belief
Eros	Greek god of physical love whose statue graces the fountain in Piccadilly Circus in London
eternal triangle	three-way relationship causing jealousy and betrayal; when two men desire one woman or vice versa
euphemism	tactful word or phrase to refer to something unpleasant or offensive, e.g. 'carnal embrace'
Eureka!	Archimedes's exclamation (meaning 'I have found it!') when his observation of the behaviour of bathwater enabled him to calculate the volume of an irregular solid; an example of **bisociation**
fabliau	short medieval tale in rhyme of a coarsely comic and satirical nature
the Fall	Adam and Eve are expelled from Paradise for succumbing to temptation and disobeying God's command not to eat the fruit of the Tree of Knowledge

farce	improbable and absurd dramatic events in a domestic setting to excite laughter; dependent on the comic timing of stage entrances and exits
figurative	using **imagery**; non-literal use of language
free will	the human power to choose between good and evil
genius loci	literally 'spirit of the place'; in mythology outdoor places were believed to be protected by such spirits; see **pantheism**
genre	type or form of writing with identifiable characteristics, e.g. detective story
Gothic	medieval **genre**, revived in late eighteenth century, concerning violence, death, horror and the supernatural; set in eerie ancient buildings and wild landscapes
Grand Tour	between 1660 and 1820 it was fashionable for English gentlemen to undertake a cultural tour of the historical sites of Europe
green world	name given to **pastoral** interludes in Shakespeare's comedies
hubris	overreaching of a human who aspires to divine power or status, resulting in downfall
hyperbole	deliberate exaggeration for effect
idiolect	style of speech peculiar to an individual character and recognisable as such
idyll	poem or prose work stressing appealing aspects of country life; Virgil imitated original Greek *Idylls* by Theocritus
imagery	descriptive language appealing to the senses; may be sustained or recurring throughout texts; **simile** or **metaphor**
innuendo	suggestive remark implying sexual misconduct
intertextuality	relationship between one text and another, e.g. *Arcadia* is connected by **theme** and event to Milton's *Paradise Lost*
irony	language intended to mean the opposite of the words expressed; amusing or cruel reversal of an outcome expected, intended or deserved; situation in which one is mocked by fate or the facts
juxtaposition	placing side by side for (ironic) contrast of interpretation
lyrical	expression of strong feelings, usually love; suggestive of music
meiosis	deliberate understatement for effect

memento mori	Latin phrase meaning 'reminder of death'; often represented symbolically in a work of art or literature
metaphor	suppressed comparison implied not stated
motif	recurring visual or acoustic feature, e.g. sound of gunshot
Nemesis	punishment for **hubris** by the goddess of retribution
non sequitur	a remark that has no relation to what has gone before
nymph	beautiful female spirit in Greek mythology; a nymphomaniac is a female who seeks sex obsessively and indiscriminately, e.g. Mrs Chater
Onan	biblical character who 'spills his seed'; onanism is an archaic synonym for masturbation
oxymoron	two contradictory terms united in a single phrase, e.g. 'a sage of lunacy'
pantheism	the belief that plural deities are to be found everywhere in nature
paradox	self-contradictory truth
paratextuality	consolidating meaning in an artistic work by referencing other arts media, e.g. using painting and/or music to enhance a literary text
parody	exaggerated imitation of style for purpose of humour and ridicule
pastoral	a literary work or picture portraying the simple, innocent and idyllic rural existence of shepherds, originating with Ancient Greek poet Theocritus in the third century as contrast to the corruption of court and city life. Marlowe's poem 'Come live with me and be my love' is a prime Elizabethan example. The presence of death in Arcadia is a subversion of this **genre**
pathos	evocation of pity for a character's suffering and helplessness
peripeteia	sudden reversal of fortune for a character, e.g. Bernard's final humiliation
philistine	person said to despise or undervalue art, beauty, intellectual thought or spiritual values; person indifferent or hostile to culture
platonic	Plato (428 BC–348 BC) was a celebrated Ancient Greek philosopher; the adjective refers to the ideal rather than the actual or the physical, as in non-sexual romantic relationships
plot	cause-and-effect sequence of events caused by characters' actions
plurality	possible multiple meanings of a text

poetic justice	rewarding of virtue and punishing of vice in fiction
postmodernism	twentieth-century literary and artistic movement that denies the existence of single, simple narratives or causes; typified by complexity, contradiction, ambiguity, diversity and interconnectedness
pun	use of word with double meaning for humorous or ironic effect
register	subset of language used for a particular purpose; language belonging to a particular social context
repartee	a ready and playful retort; witty banter
reprise	an exact repetition of an earlier scene or event
Restoration drama	comedy performed between 1660 and 1710, after the restitution of the English monarchy with Charles II; known for its bawdy action, humour and stupid characters; Lady Croom and Chater belong to this **genre**
riposte	a quick, sharp return of speech or action; counterstroke
risqué	audaciously bordering on the bawdy; slightly indecent
Romanticism	influential artistic movement of the late-eighteenth and early-nineteenth centuries, characterised by the rebellious assertion of the individual and a belief in the spiritual correspondence between man and nature
satire	exposing of vice or foolishness of a person or institution to ridicule; *Arcadia* satirises 'dons on the make'
satyr	in Greek mythology satyrs are deities of the woods and mountains; half human and half goat, they are symbolic of lechery
simile	comparison introduced by 'as' or 'like'; epic **simile** is a lengthy and detailed **analogy**
stereotype	category of person with typical characteristics, often the target for mockery, e.g. Chater as cuckold
stichomythia	dramatic technique whereby a series of short speeches is given to alternating speakers in a battle of **wits**
style	selection and organisation of language elements; typical of **genre** or individual user of language
surrealism	literary and artistic movement begun in Paris in 1924; typified by the **juxtaposition** of incongruous ideas or objects, in an attempt to express the subconscious freed from the controls of reason and narrative sequence, as in dreams
symbol	object, person or event that represents something more than itself, e.g. apple

synopsis	summary of plot
Theatre of the Absurd	movement in European theatre between the 1940s and 1960s, based on the philosophy that life is inherently without meaning
theme	abstract idea or issue explored in a text
tone	emotional aspect of the voice of a text, e.g. 'bitter', 'passionate'
tragedy	literary work traditionally concerning someone high born and gifted coming to a fatal end; characterised by waste, loss and a fall from power
Two cultures	title of an influential 1959 Rede Lecture by British scientist and novelist C. P. Snow, which discussed the unfortunate breakdown of communication between the sciences and the humanities in modern society
whodunnit	slang name for a detective story
willing suspension of disbelief	Coleridge's expression to describe how audiences do not expect rules of realism to apply to **drama** and will accept theatrical conventions as an act of 'poetic faith'
zeitgeist	German for 'the spirit of the age'

Questions & Answers

LITERATU

$$x^n + y^n = $$

Essay questions and specimen plans

Coursework titles

As there is a choice of ten Victorian novels to pair with *Arcadia*, the sample questions below leave open the title of the centre's selected novel, and also the choice of other plays studied to provide dramatic context. There is, of course, an anomaly in the inclusion of this play in the list of three drama texts specified, since *Arcadia* was neither written nor set in the Victorian period (1837–1901). A knowledge of Oscar Wilde's *The Importance of Being Earnest* would be invaluable for students as a comparable social comedy drama text.

1 Explore the ways Stoppard uses setting in *Arcadia* for dramatic effect.
Then either:
  a compare them with how other relevant plays use setting.
  Or:
  b compare the ways Stoppard uses setting in *Arcadia* with the ways … uses the environment of … in … .

2 Stoppard has 'a fascination with the interconnectedness between then and now, the unreliability of evidence, the haphazardness of what survives'. Consider this description.
Then either:
  a discuss how these preoccupations feature in *Arcadia* and other relevant plays.
  Or:
  b relate one of the elements of the quotation to both *Arcadia* and … .

Further coursework titles

3 Explore how Stoppard examines the effects of the passing of time in *Arcadia*. Compare how this theme is used in … .

4 What is *Arcadia* saying about the quest for knowledge, and how do these views relate to those of the two periods in which the play is set?

5 How does Stoppard portray women in the play? Examine the characterisation and function of the female characters, and compare them to the main female characters in … .

6 Explore the character of Septimus, showing how he develops through the play, and compare his transformation with that of … in … .

7 Do you consider *Arcadia* to be primarily a social or a domestic drama? Consider both interpretations of the play, and explain how it compares to other similar plays.

8 Write about the importance of structure in *Arcadia* and … .

9 Examine the various conflicts and tensions of a changing society presented in *Arcadia* and explain their significance for the character of Thomasina and …

10 How is the historical period relevant to the content and themes of *Arcadia* and to those of other plays you have read?

11 To what extent does *Arcadia* depict a collision of two worlds? How is this also shown in … ?

12 Discuss the presentations of same-gender and other-gender relationships in *Arcadia* and … .

13 How is social class relevant to *Arcadia* and other dramatic works you have read that are set in the nineteenth century?

Exam essays

The exemplar essay questions that follow can be used for planning practice and/or full essay writing within the time limit, with or without the text. Some essay titles are accompanied by suggestions for ideas to include in a plan.

Remember to talk about the play and the audience, not the book and the reader, and try to visualise how it would appear on stage and how it would sound; the dramatic effect is an essential element of the written text you are being asked to respond to.

If you are studying *Arcadia* for an examined open book unit, you need to know exactly which Assessment Objectives are being tested and where the heaviest weighting falls. You will probably have looked at or practised past paper questions so that you know what kind of title to expect, and it would be helpful if your teacher shared with you the examiners' reports for previous years' exams.

Exam essays should be clearly structured, briskly argued, concisely expressed, closely focused, and supported by brief but constant textual references. They should show a combination of knowledge, understanding, analysis and informed personal response. Length is not in itself an issue — quality matters rather than quantity — but you have to fulfil the assessment criteria, and without sufficient coverage and exploration of the title you cannot be awarded a top mark. Aim realistically for approximately 12 paragraphs or three to four sides of A4.

Do not take up one absolute position and argue only one interpretation; there are no 'yes' or 'no' answers in literature. The other side must have something to be said for it or the question would not have been set, so consider both views before deciding which one to argue, and mention the other one first to prove your awareness of different reader opinions and audience reactions. It is permissible to say your view is equally balanced, provided that you have explained the contradictory evidence and have proved that ambivalence is built into the text.

It is a useful class activity to role-play being examiners and to set essay titles in groups and exchange them for planning practice. This makes you think about the main issues, some perhaps not previously considered, and which scenes would lend themselves to passage-based questions. Try to get into the way of thinking like an examiner and using their kind of language for expressing titles, which must avoid vagueness and ambiguity.

Exam essay process

The secret of exam essay success is a good plan, which gives coverage and exploration of the title and refers to the four elements of text: plot, characterisation, language and themes. Think about the issues freshly rather than attempt to regurgitate your own or someone else's ideas, and avoid giving the impression of a pre-packaged essay you are determined to deliver whatever the title.

- When you have chosen a question, underline its key words and define them briefly, in as many ways as are relevant to the text to form the introduction and provide the background. Plan the rest of the essay, staying focused on the question, in approximately 12 points, recorded as short phrases with indication of support. Include a concluding point that does not repeat anything already said but that pulls your ideas together to form an overview. It may refer to other readers' opinions, refer back to the title or include a relevant quotation from the text or elsewhere.

- Check your plan to see that you have dealt with all parts of the question, have used examples of the four elements of text in your support and have analysed, not just described. Remind yourself of the Assessment Objectives (printed on the exam paper). Group points and organise the plan into a structure with numbers, brackets or arrows.

- Tick off the points in your plan as you use them in the writing of your essay and put a diagonal line through the whole plan once you have finished. You can add extra material as you write, as long as it does not take you away from the outline you have constructed.

- Concentrate on expressing yourself clearly as you write your essay and on writing accurately, concisely and precisely (e.g. 'the reference to rice pudding is humorously incongruous' is more specific than 'she is amusing when she asks about dinner'). Integrate short quotations throughout the essay.

- Allow five minutes at the end for checking and improving your essay in content and style. Insertions and crossings-out, if legible, are encouraged. As well as checking accuracy of spelling, grammar and punctuation, watch out for errors of fact, name or title slips, repetition and absence of linkage between paragraphs. Make sure your conclusion sounds conclusive, and not as though you have run out of time, ideas or ink. A few minutes spent checking can make the difference of a grade.

Planning practice

Using some of the titles from the section below, practise planning essay titles within a time limit of eight minutes, using approximately half a page. Aim for at least ten points and know how you would support them. Use numbers to structure the plan. Do this in groups and exchange and compare plans. Get used to using note form and abbreviations for names to save time. Since beginnings are the most daunting part of the essay for many students, you could also practise opening paragraphs for your planned essays. Remember to define the terms of the title, especially any abstract words, as this will give your essay breadth, depth and structure, e.g. if the word 'knowledge' appears, say exactly what you take 'knowledge' to mean and how many different things it can mean in the context of the play. Students also often find conclusions difficult, so experiment with final paragraphs for the essays you have planned. The whole essay is working towards the conclusion, so you need to know what it is going to be before you start writing the essay, and to make it clear that you have proved your case, whatever that may be.

Passage-based questions: prescribed

The question you choose may direct you to one or two prescribed passages, but you will need to show your knowledge of the whole play as well as your response to and analysis of particular sequences. Do not waste time paraphrasing what happens in the scene or is being said in the speech; just give a quick summary of its setting and context, along the lines of who is present and why, what has just happened, what will follow and what is the dramatic purpose of it.

Examiners advise that reference to the rest of the work should be as much as 60% of the essay even for a passage-based question. Focus closely on the passage(s) but also relate their content and/or language to elsewhere in the text, backwards and forwards, and link your comments to the overall themes and/or structure of the play. Include references to character, event, theme and language, and ask how the episode modifies or adds to our understanding of the play so far, and how typical it is of the work as a whole. Think about reader/audience reaction, using your own as the basis for your response.

Here are the questions to address when analysing drama text passages:
- Is it primarily looking forward to something that is to come, or looking backwards to explain or reinforce a previous event? The right answer will usually be both.
- Are there any entrances or exits, and what effect do they have if so?
- Look at stage directions. What are the effects of the positioning of props, and of the facial expressions and body movements being performed?
- Comment on the imagery and relate it to other similar or contrasting usages and its link with themes.
- Is there a dominant or silent presence or one who is given relatively few lines? How might the positions or grouping of the characters suggest support for or opposition to each other?
- Is there any irony or dramatic irony? Who knows what at this stage?

- Where is the audience's sympathy, and why?
- How does this passage relate to elsewhere? Is it similar or in contrast to another episode?
- How does the language and its tone reveal character, and how does it affect the audience's feelings about something or someone?
- How does the scene add to plot, character and theme? Why is it there?

1 **Stoppard said that in his plays 'Extreme seriousness co-exists happily with extreme frivolity.' Explain how this co-existence works in the extract from the beginning of scene 3 to Thomasina: 'I hope you die!' and her exit p. 52. Comment on the effect of this co-existence on the play as a whole.**

Possible plan:

- play is a tragi-comedy, typically postmodernist mixture of opposite genres
- Plautus sitting on top of Thomasina's lesson book is a co-existence of frivolous and serious props
- the repartee is in comic style, but the content concerns crucial issue of knowledge
- Septimus's receipt of a challenge to a duel is deadly serious, although Chater is a buffoon
- sex treated humorously but it also leads to Chater's death, desired by Brice
- Cleopatra, Byron and Dido are all tragic figures; Cleopatra is considered by history to have been a character whose frivolity caused serious consequences
- Thomasina talks about ancient cultures and loss with a mixture of passion and amusement, e.g. 'noodle' as well as 'How can we sleep for grief?'
- stage direction top of p. 48 shows Septimus really cares for Lady Croom and is therefore suffering
- Thomasina's speeches on p. 49 are serious and cover maths, death, attraction, God's creation, discovery — but end in an ironic misprophecy
- Septimus makes a long and uncharacteristically serious speech p. 50–51, but then moves to playing a joke on Thomasina
- Thomasina's mode hitherto has been teasing and flippant (though making underlying serious observations) and we expect her to react with amusement here, but instead she shows distress and anger, and exits 'in tears of rage'
- pathos of Thomasina's last moments tempered by knowledge that her discovery will be refound and proved with computers, and aspects of her will live on in her descendants, Valentine, Chloë and Gus

2 **Reread Act 1 of *Arcadia* from the opening stage directions to Septimus: 'This time you may have overreached yourself', p. 7. Consider the use made of mathematics in this extract and in the play as a whole.**

Possible plan:

- Fermat's Last Theorem used to introduce themes of mystery and lost knowledge
- treated humorously by being compared to and confused with 'carnal embrace'

- developed into link with heat, to be pursued later in the play
- jam in the rice pudding analogy introduces 'time's arrow' concept
- leads to discussion of time and free will — Newton's Laws
- Thomasina's theory applies maths to nature, predicting future and role of computers
- this scene central to Thomasina/Septimus relationship as maths teacher/pupil, an attraction that will bring them together to waltz
- Valentine's role to rediscover Thomasina's work, so maths the ancestral thread
- free will/determinism debate will continue throughout play
- maths represents classical, rational, ordered universe — until Chaos Theory
- maths v. arts (thinking v. feeling) are ways of understanding life and denoting character; but not mutually exclusive, e.g. Valentine, Septimus

3 Reread Act 2 scene 5 of *Arcadia*, from p. 82 Hannah: 'Well, I think that's everybody' to the end of the scene. Discuss how an audience might react to Hannah in this extract, and comment on her role and importance in the play as a whole.

Possible plan:
- this dialogue is an academic duel between rivals
- Hannah has right instincts and intuitions because motivated by genuine interest and not by self-aggrandisement
- carries the flag for Thomasina as an intelligent female; shares her curiosity and determination
- free of the lust that is taking the world to hell in a handcart
- her study of Caro and Sidley Park gardens links Regency to present and includes themes of death, sexual attraction, historical knowledge, cultural change
- honorary member of modern Croom family and regarded with affection by Val, Gus, Chloë and absent Hermione
- she plays role of Bernard's Nemesis: she slaps him, refuses his offer of sex and exposes him to academic ridicule by writing to *The Times*
- wins audience respect and sympathy for her commitment and integrity, and for her championship of Thomasina and Septimus
- she conveys playwright's view that we know 'Nothing' but that 'It's wanting to know that makes us matter'

4 Reread the ending of the play, from 'Septimus enters with an oil lamp', p. 122. Comment on its relationship to the rest of the play and say how satisfactory you consider it to be as an ending to a drama. Suggest how audience reactions may differ to it.

5 Look again at the opening of the play, as far as Septimus saying 'Sit!' to Plautus, p. 6. By a careful examination of this scene, consider the importance of Stoppard's presentation of the country-house context in which the action is set to your understanding of the play as a whole.

6 Look at the end of scene 3, from the stage direction *'Septimus gives up the game'*, p. 53. What does the rest of the scene show us about Septimus's state of mind at this point in the play? How does his mood here relate to his previous and later behaviour?

7 Look again at the passage in scene 2 beginning with Hannah: 'Mr Peacock?', p. 25 up to Hannah: 'You have a way with you, Bernard. I'm not sure I like it', p. 31. What effect does Bernard and Hannah's dialogue in this extract have on your thoughts and feelings towards them both?

8 Look again at Lady Croom's attack on Noakes in scene 7, from Lady Croom: 'Mr Noakes!', p. 113 to Lady Croom: 'We are intruding here…Come along sir!', p. 115. Write about its significance, concentrating on the revelation of Lady Croom's character and the play's central themes.

9 Look again at the argument between Valentine and Bernard in scene 5, from Valentine: 'I read that somewhere —', p. 79 to *'On which, Valentine leaves the room'*, p. 82. What do the dramatic situation and content of the speeches add to the themes and atmosphere of the play?

10 Look at Chloë and Valentine's dialogue at the beginning of scene 7, up to her exit, p. 98. Describe the purpose and effect of this conversation at this stage in the play, and the function of the character of Chloë in general.

11 *Arcadia* is 'a play that seems obsessed with the number three'. Discuss this view, basing your answer on the material in scene 6.

12 Using scene 4 and the characters of Hannah, Bernard and Valentine as a starting point, show how the play as a whole presents the problems and pitfalls of academic research.

13 Stoppard's creative aim is 'the perfect marriage of ideas and high comedy'. Discuss whether you think he has achieved this aim in *Arcadia*, including in your answer an analysis of the opening of scene 2, as far as Hannah's entrance on p. 25.

14 Explore Stoppard's presentation of love and sexual attraction in the play, including in your answer an examination of the dialogue between Thomasina and Septimus in scene 1, p. 2 up to the entrance of Jellaby on p. 5, and of the dialogue between Hannah and Chloë in scene 2, from Bernard's exit on p. 44 to the end of the scene.

15 Reread Valentine's long speech on page 62. Explain the ideas and views he is expressing, and say how they connect to the themes and events of the play.

16 Stoppard has said: 'My plays are convergences of different threads.' With reference to the extract in scene 7 from *'Lord Augustus, fifteen years old…'*, p. 102 to *'Pause. Two researchers again'*, p. 105, examine how he achieves convergence.

17 Stoppard has claimed 'My distinguishing mark is an absolute lack of certainty about almost anything.' Discuss the concept of certainty in the play, including reference to the first half of scene 5, as far as Bernard: 'And he killed Chater', p. 79.

Sample essays

Below are two sample essays of different types written by different students. Both of them have been assessed as falling within the top band. You can judge them against the Assessment Objectives for this text for your exam board and decide on the mark you think each deserves and why. You may also be able to see ways in which each could be improved in terms of content and style.

Sample essay 1

Reread Valentine's long speech on p. 62. Explain the ideas and views he is expressing, and say how they connect to the themes and events of the play.

Valentine is a key character in the play, because he acts as the nexus which connects the events of the two periods and makes the scientific and mathematical ideas accessible to the present-day generation of humanities scholars. He also, of course, plays that role for the audience in the theatre, most of whom can be expected to know very little about Newtonian physics and thermodynamics, and probably have at best a hazy and populist notion of what 'Chaos Theory' is.

He is, however, not a cipher. He is able to bridge the two worlds (arguably, the four worlds: two of time, two of temperament) precisely because he does have an artistic and creative streak as well as a scientist's rigour. Perhaps the most surprising element of his uncharacteristically protracted speech on p. 62 is when he says 'It makes me so happy'. This is the credo of the true scientist, but much more it is the belief of a creative artist forced to look at the world afresh. This is the only time we see Valentine being passionate; he gets angry with Bernard for being disparaging about science and scientists, but here he is being positive, and it makes the audience see him differently, as a tortoise coming out of his shell.

Valentine's speech begins with an explanation of the mathematics underlying the Mandelbrot set of fractal images, one of the central themes of the play: 'If you knew the algorithm and fed it back say ten thousand times…'. Fractal images were discovered by mathematicians investigating 'iterative functions', ones in which the value derived from a starting point is 'fed…back' to be the starting point of the next calculation. This can be repeated an infinite number of times, and if the resulting function is depicted graphically the effect is of 'zooming in' on part of the image. But what makes these images truly remarkable is that they achieve what Thomasina, the mathematical prodigy of the earlier part of the play, can only speculate upon: that there could be 'an equation for nature'. Until the discovery of fractals, it was thought that the complex forms of most living organisms were beyond the power of mathematics to describe, and this was seen as a profound limitation upon the ability of mathematicians to encapsulate reality. Fractals removed that limitation, in the same way as Chaos Theory, which is related to them, allowed mathematics for the first time to explain and predict other forms of complex natural phenomena. Valentine summarises this: 'We're better at predicting events at the edge of the galaxy or inside the nucleus of an atom than whether it'll rain on auntie's garden party three Sundays from now.'

Valentine's view, though, is not that Chaos Theory will finally resolve this old conundrum, but rather one closer to Thomasina's: even with the most advanced algorithms deriving from this field (and his own of population biology), natural phenomena will always be so complex that they will defy human prediction: 'The future is disorder', he says, and 'the weather will always be unpredictable'. This is a form of humility in the face of nature. But he draws a different conclusion from that of Thomasina (which drives Septimus to insanity in the hermitage), that they face a bleak future of the doomed universe growing cold; rather, it allows him to feel exhilarated in the face of the uncertainty. And this is where he reveals his unusual colours: whereas most scientists crave certainty and all-embracing explanations, he actually revels in the impossibility of achieving this goal. He rather shares the philosophical view of Karl Popper, which is that all that scientists do is offer a provisional theory which is thought to be true until it is disproved and replaced by a better one. 'A door like this has cracked open five or six times since we got up on our hind legs', he says, neatly summarising the intellectual history of the human race; these are the times when the old certainties give way and the road is open for the truly visionary thinker to come up with a new paradigm. He wants to be one of those, hence his belief that 'It's the best possible time to be alive, when almost everything you thought you knew is wrong.'

Clearly, these ideas relate to many of the central concerns of the play. One important strand is Thomasina's emergence as a mathematical genius, and her pioneering work, which is tragically cut off by the fire that killed her on the eve of her seventeenth birthday. It is possible for the audience to feel somewhat confused by the mathematical and physical concepts that are introduced in rapid succession in the early part of the play, and Valentine's role is to help the audience to understand them by spelling them out for the benefit of Bernard and, particularly, Hannah. Thomasina has two concerns: the first is with Newton, determinism and the reversibility of phenomena — why you can't stir the jam apart — and the conclusion, reinforced by the Second Law of Thermodynamics, that the universe must therefore inevitably run down and die as light and heat are extinguished. The second is her attempt to produce an equation for nature — a forerunner of Mandelbrot, iterative functions and fractal images. This latter relates directly to Valentine's work on population biology, also inspired by the Sidley Park estate (game books in his case, apple leaves in hers), which relies on the mathematics of Chaos Theory, which in turn derives from iterative functions. This is the intellectual link that holds the play together, a parallel to the emotional links that tie the characters to one another across the divide of time; Valentine is fond of Hannah, who is fond of Thomasina, who is Valentine's forebear. That Bernard and Valentine do not get on is symptomatic of Bernard's arrogant intolerance and lack of true intellectual values.

Valentine's speech also stands in interesting contrast to the other large-scale set-piece speech of the play, Bernard's rehearsal in scene 5 of the talk he intends to give to reveal his 'discovery' about Chater's fate and Byron's disappearance. Hannah, an intelligent and sympathetic audience, allows Valentine to deliver his thoughts uninterrupted — because he knows what he is talking about, and has given careful consideration to his argument. Bernard, by contrast, leaping from limited evidence to unjustified conclusions, is repeatedly and rightly interrupted. So this speech of Valentine, and its reception, can also be seen as another piece of evidence for Stoppard's subtle support in the play for true scholarship over superficiality and sensationalism, and also for the intellectual views being expressed in the speech.

Sample essay 2

The ending of *Arcadia* has been described as a 'surprising and moving resolution'. Look at the ending from p. 124 '*Septimus and Valentine study the diagram doubled by time*', and discuss the ways in which it is or is not surprising, moving and a resolution.

Since the play is full of mysteries, several of which remain unsolved, it is consistent and not surprising that the play ends with the audience not knowing what is really going on in the relationship between Septimus and Thomasina. He kisses her now, and has kissed her previously in the notorious gazebo/hermitage/cottage, the place in the garden for sexual liaison for every age, but here he refuses to go to her bedroom. However, we do not know whether he relents after the action of the play, and we do not know how Thomasina sets fire to her room with the candle Septimus lights for her, so the mystery continues. This, unsurprisingly, confirms the theme of not ever being able to know what really happened, even if you were there. Lady Croom will never know her own daughter's feelings for her tutor and probably not even the real cause of her death. Given that humans are always full of surprises, nothing they can do would be surprising, and Septimus has been an enigmatic character throughout the play in any case. We do not know what his real feelings are towards his schoolfriend, Lord Byron, or why he is so strongly attracted to Lady Croom, let alone what he really feels about his pupil. It is perhaps surprising that the apparently proper Septimus appears to have been so unprofessional in the gazebo, with both Mrs Chater and Thomasina, yet as Chloë points out, what goes 'wrong is people fancying people who aren't supposed to be in that part of the plan', or as Valentine scientifically puts it: 'The attraction that Newton left out', since it is unpredictable and incapable of rational explanation.

What is moving about the ending is that the more attractive, intelligent and sensitive characters come together in pairs and share a romantic interlude across the time divide. We feel sorry for Gus and Hannah, both social misfits to a certain extent, and enjoy their final tender moment of mutual appreciation, even as we know that their relationship will not develop any further. Even more do we feel moved by the teacher/pupil duo because of the imminent tragedy awaiting Thomasina, and by extension Septimus, whose life will also be ruined by it. That we know and they do not adds a complicity and poignancy for the

audience; as in a pantomime, we feel we should warn them of an evil standing behind them. One cannot but be moved by the pathos of a potentially brilliant life cut short on the eve of its seventeenth birthday. The periods and personalities merge in the pairs of waltzers who are the champions of the best of humanity in both ages; we feel they touch each other, and therefore they touch us.

The ending is a resolution in that it is a 'convergence of different threads', which Stoppard likes to structure into his plays. Although the audience find it unsatisfactory that there is no real ending and nothing is actually resolved, it is Stoppard's aim, in accordance with postmodernism, to defeat audience expectations, and his regular audience would not expect anything different. To balance the frustration that the ending is elusive, that the story does not end as desired or predicted — or in line with the dictates of comedy — there is the appreciation that this is more realistic, being an ending full of irony and uncertainty, and it does have a discernible pattern, even symmetry, a satisfying integrity with the rest of the play, and a genre-defying mingling of comic and tragic dramatic elements. It performs a neatly circular dance movement: the play begins with a discussion of carnal embrace and ends with an act of carnal embrace; now Thomasina 'is old enough to have a carcass of her own'. The dance teases us that their relationship may blossom, yet we know it cannot, despite the attraction between bodies and minds that obviously exists, and this is a comment on life's tragic ironies and the defeat of human desires.

The piano is a symbol of logical sequence and harmonious order — like its scientific counterpart, the computer — and the waltz music brings two people together as one. But there is another set of imagery in the play, that of destruction in the form of fire and guns; one is layered over the other in this ending, just as the whole play is a series of layers. Hannah and Gus are the modern overlay on top of 1812, like Mr Noakes's before and after sketch book designs of the garden. We would like to think that Hannah and Gus will be able to carry the torch for Thomasina and Septimus, according to the latter's theory that what is shed and lost will be found and picked up again.

Further study

As the best-known living English playwright, Tom Stoppard has been the subject of a number of critical works. Good starting points are:

Hayman, R. (1977) *Tom Stoppard* (Contemporary Playwrights), Heinemann.

Hunter, J. (2000) *Tom Stoppard: Rosencrantz and Guildenstern Are Dead, Jumpers, Travesties, Arcadia* (Faber Critical Guides), Faber.

Kelly, K. E. (ed.) (2001) *The Cambridge Companion to Tom Stoppard*, Cambridge University Press.

Other books that will enable the student to pursue particular aspects of the play are:

Byatt, A. S. (1990) *Possession*, Chatto and Windus.

Eisler, B. (1999) *Byron: Child of Passion, Fool of Fame*, Hamish Hamilton.

Gleick, J. (1987) *Chaos: Making a New Science*, Viking.

Hall, N. (ed.) (1992) *'New Scientist' Guide to Chaos*, Penguin.

Hawkins, H. (1995) *Strange Attractors: Literature, Culture and Chaos Theory*, Harvester Wheatsheaf.

Kiernan, V. G. (1988) *The Duel in European History: Honour and the Reign of Aristocracy*, Oxford University Press.

Koestler, A. (1964) *The Act of Creation*, Hutchison.

MacCarthy, F. (2002) *Byron: Life and Legend*, John Murray.

Mandelbrot, B. B. (1982) *The Fractal Geometry of Nature*, W. H. Freeman.

Peacock, T. L. (1815) *Headlong Hall*, Oxford University Press.

Singh, S. (1997) *Fermat's Last Theorem*, Fourth Estate.

Walpole, H. (1764) *The Castle of Otranto*, Penguin.

General internet resources

- http://rhsweb.org/library/arcadia.htm is an outstanding set of links.
- www.cherwell.oxon.sch.uk/arcadia/outline0.htm is a useful introduction.
- www.courttheatre.org/home/plays/0607/arcadia/playnotes/Glossary.doc is a useful glossary of references.
- http://faculty.uccb.ns.ca/philosophy/arcadia/frontpage.htm is another useful set with documents and links.
- http://faculty.uccb.ns.ca/philosophy/arcadia/dictionary.htm has 'The Arcadia Dictionary'.
- http://teachers.edenpr.org/~rolson/ArcadiaWeb/ is another good introductory site.
- www.longferry.co.uk/arcadia/arcadiap1.html has photographs of the City of Oxford Theatre Guild website about *Arcadia*.
- www.skidmore.edu/academics/lsi/arcadia/index.html is a study guide on the play.
- www.skidmore.edu/academics/theater/productions/arcadia/ is a mirror of the same guide.
- www.sondheimguide.com/Stoppard/links.html is a useful list of links.
- www.sondheimguide.com/Stoppard/secbiblio.html is a detailed Stoppard bibliography.

Specific internet resources

A series of three useful scholarly articles on aspects of the play are as follows (the first and third are by Burkhard Niederhoff, the other by Anja Müller-Muth):

- www.uni-tuebingen.de/uni/nec/niederhoff111.htm 'Fortuitous wit: dialogue and epistemology in Tom Stoppard's *Arcadia*'.
- www.uni-tuebingen.de/uni/nec/mue-mu1223.htm is Anja Müller-Muth's response: 'It's wanting to know that makes us matter'.

- www.uni-tuebingen.de/uni/nec/niederhoff1312.htm is his reply, 'Who shot the hare in Stoppard's *Arcadia*?'

- www.arionpress.com/images/matthews/gallery62.html relates to an edition of the play published in 2001 by Arion Press, containing four watercolours by William Matthews that show four stages of the evolution of the house and gardens.
- www.ams.org/notices/199511/arcadia.pdf is an article entitled 'Love and the second law of thermodynamics'.
- www.siam.org/news/news.php?id=727 is an interview with Robert Osserman about maths in *Arcadia*.
- www.skidmore.edu/academics/theater/productions/arcadia/byron.html is an article about Byron and *Arcadia*.
- http://math.bu.edu/DYSYS/arcadia/ is 'Chaos, fractals, and Arcadia'.
- www.fortunecity.com/emachines/e11/86/mandel.html is the full text of Benoit Mandelbrot's important article 'Fractals — a geometry of nature'.
- http://en.wikipedia.org/wiki/Timeline_of_thermodynamics%2C_statistical_mechanics%2C_and_random_processes is a timeline of thermodynamics.
- http://engphil.astate.edu/gallery/Trelawn.html is the text of Trelawny's *Recollections*, which throws light on the life of Byron.
- http://faculty.uccb.ns.ca/philosophy/arcadia/library1.htm is a source of Anne Barton's essay 'Twice around the grounds'.
- The text of the *Cambridge Companion to Stoppard* is now available (in part) on Google Books:
  http://books.google.com/books?id=RWCYlI2jrGgC&pg=PA33&lpg=PA33&dq=%22felicity+kendal%22+stoppard&source=web&ots=iDNEMnD6TS&sig=69Pr2gXXWZKkKDLU5LlzZpnJ900#PPR9,M1 Unfortunately, the essays on *Arcadia* are not available, so the original book will need to be used.